Fathers Aren't Supposed to Die

Five Brothers Reunite to Say Good-bye

T. M. Shine

Simon & Schuster

New York   London   Sydney   Singapore

SIMON & SCHUSTER
Rockefeller Center
1230 Avenue of the Americas
New York, NY 10020

SIMON & SCHUSTER and colophon are registered trademarks
of Simon & Schuster, Inc.

Designed by Chris Welch
Manufactured in the United States of America

1   3   5   7   9   10   8   6   4   2

Library of Congress Cataloging-in-Publication Data
Shine, T. M.
Fathers aren't supposed to die : five brothers reunite to
say good-bye / T. M. Shine.
p. cm.
1. Death—Social aspects—Case studies. 2. Parents—Death—Case studies.
3. Fathers—Death—Case studies. 4. Adult children—Psychology—Case
studies. 5. Shine, T. M. 6. Sons—Biography. I. Title.
HQ1073 .S53 2000   306.89 21—dc21   99-043536
ISBN 0-684-86351-0

To Family

Acknowledgments

Much appreciation to Jill Reed, Earl Bronsteen, Jane Musgrave, Bob (Weinberg) & Jake (Cline), the Walsh family, Michael Farver, Dave Hogerty, Mark Gauert, Greg Carannante, Tom Swick, Andy & Nancy, Laura Werder, W.A. Baum Co., Sister Margaret McGill, Ray Recchi, Roger McGrath, David Rosenthal, Steve & Janet Head, Nicole Graev, *City Link*, Mike "Michael" Redmond, Nick Cave, Colleen Dougher-Telcik, Geoffrey Kloske, Will O'Shaughnessy, Pat & Belle Sama, Sharon Ives, Punter & Punter Jr., Dave Warm, and Jim Virga. And thanks always to Tom Shroder, Dave Barry, Stu Purdy, Robin Doussard, Al Hart, and Johnny "99" Hughes.

Fathers Aren't Supposed to Die

Part I

"One can no more look steadily at death than at the sun."
—La Rochefoucauld

Too many dogs loose this morning.

These early runs have become so regimented—the nod to the crossing guard by the elementary school, going wide by the corner of Ocean Avenue to avoid the sprinklers, breathing deep before the steep incline on Drew Street— that I usually welcome the chase, the bark, the growl, the shouts of the owner.

But not today. Every time I have to lift my head, skid off course, drop my speed, it distracts me from the beeper in my hand. When I bought this thing I didn't get one of those belt clips and these silly running shorts have no pockets, so I thought about leaving it at home, thought about how twenty minutes or a half hour wouldn't make a difference.

But I want it to make a difference, damn it. And besides, it's doctor's orders.

"Someone in the family needs to have a pager and keep it in their possession at all times," the doctor had said. "There will be urgent questions that have to be answered, things you need to know right away."

But all the questions have been answered now, and there is only one thing left to know. Only one beep remains, and last night I was playing around with the gadget's options. Do I want *diddly-deet*, an air-drill shrill, a simple *blip* . . . *blip* . . . for this final page? What should be the signal for death?

I chose the silent vibrator mode. If it goes off in the next second, a shiver will spread from my palm, trail up the nerves of my arm, and then jolt down my spine until my whole body is numb.

My father will be dead.

And I am ready. I am on the brink of acceptance.

Old people are supposed to die, I said in a whisper of resignation two nights ago. "Yeah, but fathers aren't," my brother Bill responded.

And I know what he is saying. He's trying to separate our impending loss from the ugliness of death itself. We have talked so much about death lately. From camping out in the ICU to calling doctors killers to debating living wills to questioning God to picking out a shiny box to lower some-one into the grimy ground, we have become entrenched in it. At one point, it prompted me to say aloud, "My life . . . is death."

This is all new to me. I know there are others like myself who have led semi-charmed lives and often find themselves saying, "No one close to me has ever died." Even the aunt you treasured when you were nine waits to die until you're thirty-one and haven't seen her in eleven years. It's a death cushion. The tragedy, the devastation, the dropping to your knees in anguish never comes. You are spared.

This story is about not being spared. It's about when the tragedy, the devastation, the dropping to your knees in anguish comes. It's about reaching the brink of acceptance and then being slammed by death in ways you couldn't possibly have fathomed.

I keep going back to that moment with the beeper cra-dled in my palm as if it were the present because I haven't accepted much since. I sometimes run it all backward, sub-tracting each thing that happened by the week, by the day, by the hour . . . but I can never seem to erase the first phone call. The one that comes with a ring of camouflage—could be the dry cleaners, could be the finance department trying to verify something on your expense report, could be the security guard downstairs notifying you that your lunch order has arrived.

Or it could be the trapdoor that drops you into your first hard lesson in death, American style.

Day One

The ring is circling around my desk, but I am deep in thought.

I can't stop thinking about what Fiona Apple had said in a magazine article about her eating disorder—"There was a time when I couldn't eat things that I felt clashed with what I was wearing"—and I am wondering, What goes with tuna?

One, two, three rings . . . catch it just before the voice mail picks up. It's either a bad connection or the voice is . . . "It's me, your brother Bill."

Even though he only lives twenty miles away I haven't seen my older brother Bill in years. But it's not about that. "Dad is in the hospital and he didn't want to tell everybody and everything was supposed to be OK but now . . . *bleeding . . . in the brain . . . he can't talk . . .*"

"I am on my way," I say.

I mechanically walk out of my cubicle and watch my feet make the square turns to my boss's desk where I stop abruptly and say those short sentences that can never be debated: "My father's in the hospital. I have to go."

"Terry, if there's anything we can—"

But my back is already turned and I'm out the door and into the elevator, dropping the twelve floors to the parking lot.

I am notorious for being an extremely slow walker. When people walk with me through the city they are sometimes in the middle of a conversation with me when they turn around and are shocked to see I am a block away. But that is nothing compared to the pace I'm setting now as I head toward the car. Lost in the thought of what has happened, I am creeping.

The hospital is an hour away from my office in Fort Lauderdale. Heading north on I-95 the highway is flanked by baby palm trees, their trunks reinforced by planks of timber until they're strong enough to stand on their own. My eyes flicker at the tropical fence then dart from car to car.

I've joked in the past that the reason I never honk my horn or swear at drivers is because even if they do something stupid on the road I don't know what's going on in their lives—maybe they just lost their job, maybe their dog just died.

Maybe their father's brain is bleeding . . .

I can hear my father's voice. Now that someone has told me he can't talk, I can hear everything he ever said. It's coming in ridiculous sound bites. "If you can touch it, you can catch it," he'd say every time a football skipped off the tips of my fingers. His arm is cocked. "Banana in!" I hear him shouting. I can see the spiral coming.

He is framed in the doorway to his bathroom thirty years ago. I am curled up on the end of his bed and he is flapping a *Reader's Digest* under his armpits to dry a fresh coat of Mennen's wet and sticky deodorant. "It's the perfect size for this." He grins.

I have screwed up big time, and he has only one thing to say: "Terry, why can't you just do what you're supposed to do?"

A horn blares. I can see in my sideview mirror that I'm running the small white car beside me off the road. I am thankful for the blast.

This ride up the highway is much too easy. I know I am driving in that space between bad and worse news. I want the traffic to jam up; I want to see brake lights; I want a milk tanker to jackknife, spilling a river of white that will tie us all up for hours. I want the whole world to be in collusion with my trepidation. But there's no stopping this. I'm being carried along like debris on fast water . . . going, going, gone, gone, gone.

And the flow quickens at the hospital. Wrought-iron security gates surround the urban hospital in West Palm Beach, but it is as welcoming as a theme-park castle. Bold signs pave the way, arrows can't be missed, smiling security guards in golf carts offer rides from the parking lot.

I walk rigidly, still trying to slow things down, but the big doors slide open while I'm ten paces away—pulling me through—and the receptionist hands off a visitor's badge as if it's the baton in a relay race.

The walls in the hallways are water blue up to my waist and then pale white to the ceiling. At the first corner there is a life-size wood carving of a graceful woman holding a baby. The baby is holding a rose.

My stride doesn't break until I reach the second-floor unit. "It's a step down from critical. The first stop after intensive care," a nurse informs me as I walk toward my father's room.

The moment I see him lying there my eyes avert to the TV high above him; it's tuned to one of those networks that specializes in syndicated oldies. *McCloud* is on.

I look back at my father. In our family I am the one who most resembles him. We both suffer from what I call Dick Van Patten disease, the most profound characteristics being a fat face and skinny legs.

Those legs are sticking out, and as I go to his side his head turns, but his stare is blank, the face is drawn. The blue-checkered gown is hanging off his broad shoulders like a low-cut blouse. I fumble with it, trying to cover his freckled skin, but it keeps sliding down.

I don't know what to say.

The last time we talked we didn't talk. It was Merry Christmas/Happy New Year/See you later. So I think of the time before when he called me out of nowhere to come up and see some senior golf tournament at PGA National in nearby Palm Beach Gardens. My interest in golf is zero, but it was a beautiful day and when I arrived I saw Chi Chi Rodriguez in a blazing red shirt, chasing another player across the greens and jabbing his putter like a sword. My father bought me a lemonade and then asked me if I would like a pretzel.

"Terry, would you like a pretzel?"

"Yes, Daddy, I would like a pretzel."

I felt like a child. I am sure it was unintentional, but the outing reminded me that although our contact of late has been nothing more than feeble phone calls and holiday hugs, we had a past and it was filled with glorious days like this. Days on Long Island that were steeped in action more than sentiment: chasing the turtles the Indians raced at Jones Beach; cheering the spin of the red, white, and blue ball of the ABA when the Nets played at the Nassau Coliseum; following the curve of a banana in toward the lamppost that was already lighting up the dusk and reaching, reaching . . .

At the PGA tournament I recall cutting across to the eighteenth hole and having to walk through a pile of gravel. Both of us were unsteady, and I wanted to use it as an excuse to reach out and grab his hand, as if we needed an excuse to hold hands. But I didn't do it.

I look down at his bed. He looks so helpless. What a horrible excuse.

I grab his hand.

In a Doctor's Minute

His hand squeezes back, but I'm not sure if it's a reflex or he knows I'm here.

I'm here, Dad.

"You're here," a voice behind me says. It is my brother Bill, but he looks so different. "You might want to call me Will," he says.

I stare at him strangely. He looks like Neil Young going to an early-bird dinner: long black hair and flip-up shades atop a striped leisure shirt, khaki pants with a woven belt, and questionable shoes. "You're dressed like a forty-year-old man," I say.

"I am a forty-year-old man," he says, not looking up.

Our greeting is over, his eyes are down on a scrap of paper. "Dad was trying to tell me something important. He couldn't talk but he was trying to write and we were going through the alphabet and this is as far as we got," he says, hoarding the paper close to his belly.

He is clenching its corners tightly and his hands are trembling. The scribbled sentence is indecipherable.

"There is enough . . ." it begins and then trails off. Seeing my father's state now I am furious that he was able to put words together a short while ago. I should have been here.

"He was set to come home Friday. He was set to come

home Friday," Bill keeps repeating as if he wants to drill it into my mind as deeply as it is embedded in his.

"What the hell happened? How long has he been here?" I ask.

Bill pushes his hair out of his face and squints up at me from behind his glasses. From as far back as I can remember it always seemed as if his eyeglass prescription was never strong enough. "Terry," he says, as if he's seeing me for the first time, as if I am new. Bill was always the most sensitive in our family, the one who took bad news the hardest, whether it was the loss of a pet or an assassination shown on the TV. I always wondered if my feelings were inadequate because his were so strong. Now, seeing him struggle for the words brings that all back.

The details he gives me are brief and convoluted. Dad had been having bad headaches, then his voice started to slur a bit. "He couldn't remember the PIN number for his ATM card," Bill says.

"He couldn't remember his PIN number?" I repeat, as if that is the most telling symptom, as if that is how they knew something was really wrong.

He'd walked into the hospital a few days earlier. They found a subdural hematoma—blood between the brain and the skull. He went into surgery, the neurologist drained it, and that was that.

"He was sitting up and eating steak the next day," Bill says.

He had called my mother, who is unable to get out

because of her own health, at home. "I miss you so much," he said.

"He was coming home Friday. Dad, you were coming home Friday," Bill says. "Tell Terry; Terry's here."

Why didn't you guys tell me he was in the hospital?

"You know Dad," Bill says.

I did. When he had gone in for a pacemaker he didn't tell anybody until he was out. He loved to mention things like that nonchalantly after the fact. "Oh, did I tell you I went into the hospital for a pacemaker last Tuesday. Zip, zip, and that was it. Amazing what they can do."

I can picture how he would have been telling me this story a week from today. "Oh, did I tell you about the brain surgery? They just put two little holes at the base of the skull and drained the blood right out. Amazing what they can do."

Nobody can seem to do anything now.

He rises from the bed in a seizure. His eyes are flickering, his limbs flailing. The nurse, a big blond guy named Andy wearing deep purple scrubs, says they've been giving him medication for the seizures but it's not working.

We ask what is happening in his head during the seizures but Andy doesn't know. How can they let him rattle his head around like this so soon after brain surgery? Shouldn't his head be strapped down or stabilized or something, *or something*?

"I don't know," Andy says sincerely. The doctor is supposed to call in a couple of minutes.

A doctor's minute is the antithesis of the New York minute. Time is racing by. When is the doctor coming? We don't know what to do with ourselves. We're measuring the minutes between seizures as if they're labor contractions. We don't know what else to do.

"That was three and a half minutes since the last one," I tell Andy when he pops in.

"OK," he says.

While waiting for the doctor, the hospital staff somehow decides to transport him to a room nearer the nurses' station so he can be monitored more closely. "I won't be your nurse anymore," Andy says.

Good-bye, Andy.

The Jell-O Story

"Hi," Andy says.

The nurse who was supposed to take over had told Andy she didn't know how to handle a patient like my father.

"I don't either but I'm going to try," Andy says.

We look at my father. We look at Andy. We look at each other.

Where's the doctor?

"He's supposed to call in a couple of minutes," Andy says.

A nurse's aide brings in some of my father's things from the other room, including a stack of envelopes.

"They're Dad's bills from home," Bill says. "He thought he'd have time to write out some checks while he was sitting around here."

I don't know what to do with myself so I start going through the bills. Cable is overdue.

My oldest brother, Danny, arrives from Port St. Lucie wearing a new buzz cut and one of his usual sweatsuits, sleeves rolled up displaying the tattoos he got before they were fashionable. He doesn't waste time asking any of the questions I did—what happened, why wasn't I told? He just goes right to my father's side and begins working on him like a therapeutic Tony Little. "OK, guy, we can get through this. Can you move your arms and legs? Let's do it!

"What are you doing with Dad's checkbook?" Danny says.

"I'm going to pay some bills," I say.

"Man, if Dad saw you with his checkbook he'd snap out of this so . . . Dad, Terry has your checkbook."

Huge chunks of time are just dropping away now. I look up and *Quincy* is on.

Danny is hearing his own sound bites. "Remember how we always had trouble with the plumbing at home?" he says. "I keep hearing Dad knocking on the bathroom door and saying, 'Whatever you do, don't flush.' "

We take turns holding his hand. . . . *The doctor will be*

with you in a couple of minutes. . . . We're getting a bit delirious ourselves.

"I'm going to get something to eat," Danny says. "You want something?"

"Anything's OK," I say.

"Don't do that to me. What do you want?" he says.

"Something that matches my clothes," I say. He looks me over, focusing on my faded black jeans and striped shirt, and says, "I'll be right back."

On account of a motorcycle accident, Danny has a slight limp that is barely noticeable unless he is tense and in a hurry. As I watch him rush out of the room, it is very noticeable.

Another seizure comes and I grip my father's arm tightly. We are arm wrestling. Even though this is when he seems most far away, it is also when he seems most alive. His blue eyes are glazed, but at least they are open. His face warps into every expression I've ever known.

Danny's back. "I'm telling you, even when Dad gets better I'm still coming back to the hospital for these Danishes," he says, wiping his mouth. "This is the best Danish I've ever gotten out of a vending machine."

Andy comes in and asks us if our father is a mouth breather. One who regularly breathes through his mouth instead of his nose. "I think I read somewhere that Michael Jordan is a mouth breather," I tell Danny, just in case he knows that my father is a mouth breather but is reluctant to admit it.

"So," Danny says.

Andy is waiting patiently but we have no definitive answer.

He's still waiting.

"We've never known him to be a mouth breather," I blurt.

Andy leaves, but then pops right back. "Oh, the doctor will be with you in a couple of minutes," he says.

The doctor is with us. "The CAT scan is showing some gunk on the outside of the brain," he says.

"What do you mean, gunk?" I ask, assuming he's trying to simplify it for us.

"You know, *gunk*," he says.

He explains little other than that our father is getting worse and we need to sign for another surgery immediately.

An orderly comes to transport him to the operating room and we follow in a strange parade out into the hallway. I'm dragging the IV stand, my hand gripped in the center of the metal pole, my arm as stiff as a majorette clenching a baton, Danny is clearing a path down the busy corridor as the orderly steers the bed in a straight line toward the elevators.

Suddenly my father jolts up. He's a child waking in the backseat of a moving car. His face is startled and he is sputtering again. I try to hold his head still. The orderly says: "Whoa, what's this all about?"

"We're used to it," Bill says.

"Nobody told me about this," she says, putting her hands up and abandoning us.

She leaves us standing there in the hallway until we become an obstacle. Hospital traffic is veering around us. A nurse approaches as if she's coming to the rescue but then she passes by in a blur. Our father has become the shopping cart with the bad wheel that nobody wants. I start to move him but I have no idea which way to go. The orderly returns but only to relate the news: "I'm sorry, but I'm not trained to deal with that."

On the strike of *that*, her eyes land on my father, and I want her to just go away now. Leave us here, we will find our way, just leave us alone.

We pull him off to the shoulder of the road and wait until another nurse, wearing a scrub top that is a cascade of multicolored balloons, walks up without a word and takes control.

Without a word, we follow.

We linger in the waiting area outside intensive care as they wheel him into surgery. There are rows and rows of scratched yellow plastic bucket seats, all attached to each other—linking one person to the next. A dark-haired, matronly woman turns to tell us her brother, a reverend, was in an accident with the church van. "My father was a preacher, and five of my brothers are preachers and three of their children are preachers," she says.

"That's a lot of preachers," I say.

We move to three chairs outside the operating room and sit silently for a short eternity.

"Remember when Dad took us all out to eat at the Old House restaurant around Christmas," Danny breaks in.

We all do but no one responds. "We must have sat at the table for two hours, but when we were leaving I went to duck in the bathroom," Danny says. "And he was coming out at the same time and he said, 'Hi, Dan,' like he was so damn glad to see me. I mean, we'd only been apart for a couple of minutes and he was glad to see me all over again.

"Hi, Dan."

Suddenly the doctor comes out and almost shoots right by us. One of us sort of sticks out a foot to trip him, and he stops short. "Oh, there you are," he says.

The surgical mask still hanging off his chin, he tells us our father survived the operation and now we'll just have to see. We don't know what questions to ask, and he's not giving up much more.

What are his chances?

"Some patients surprise me," he says.

Is that what it's going to take? My brothers look at each other. How far is the distance between a surprise and a miracle?

The more questions we ask, the more steps backward the doctor takes. Then he cocks his head and tells a story about another patient who had gunk on the brain. "And after I removed it he was fine," he says. (We like that. That sounds encouraging.) "Then, a day later, the brain collapsed like Jell-O."

The doctor flips his wrist to look at a watch that isn't there, puts the mask back in place, and quickly leaves. Back in the direction only he's allowed to go.

Danny squeezes my knee, and we all rise and walk up the corridor toward the lobby. "There it is, F4," Danny says, pointing at the Danish as we pass the vending machines.

There is a large group of about thirty people holding vigil for the preacher outside the ICU. The matronly woman is leading them in song. Her church-grown voice is sweet, and it is a graceful hymn. The others join in a chorus of heaven's virtues and what a beautiful place it must be. They sound so strong.

I feel so weak.

Turning into the lobby, we pick up our pace. "Are you going to hand in your visitor's badge?" Bill asks.

"What for?" I say as we pass the front desk.

The electronic doors swish open, and we are out into the night. We break off to go to our cars.

Danny stops, turns, and says: "Why did he have to tell us that Jell-O story?"

"I don't know," I say. "People tell stories."

And we just stand there for what seems like a doctor's minute. The whole day is crashing around us.

"Is tomorrow Friday?" Bill says. "He was supposed to go home on Friday."

Free Fall

Nothing's changed.

He just lies there.

Everything's changed. No one goes to work, no one goes to the store, no one makes any plans other than to be at our father's bedside. We've become hospital rats.

By day two, we know where the best soda machine is (it has Fresca). By day three, we're no longer using the pay phone but making free calls from deep inside nursing station B2. By day four, we know who the good nurses are (they're so much smarter here in ICU) and the bad (here comes the bitch). By day five, Bill somehow knows what kind of car every doctor drives: the neurosurgeon has an STS Cadillac Seville, the cardiologist a classic Corvette, the internist a GMC Yukon. "But I think it's his wife's," Bill says. He's got an eye for that kind of thing. By day six, we know orderlies' hobbies. "Gerard flies those radio-controlled airplanes. The big ones."

But we know no more about my father's condition. "He hasn't plateaued yet," one doctor says.

We think that's a good thing but then we second-guess ourselves. Can you plateau downward?

After the surgery, it was all about the swelling going down. "The brain has been through two surgeries within a week," the doctor said. "Once the swelling goes down we'll see where we're at."

Well, the swelling must have gone down by now, but we don't see a thing.

We continue to occupy ourselves with the mundane. Going through Dad's bills, Danny finds out our parents are supporting one of those Sally Struthers–type kids in Trinidad. But Danny swears he recognizes the name from decades ago when they first started it. "This kid must be fifty now and we're still sending her cookie money," he says.

Bill has been personalizing the room, bringing in photos and hanging up an article from a Valley Stream, New York, newspaper that recently chronicled my father's feats during World War II. The historical society in his hometown had asked him for some memorabilia for an upcoming exhibit on the war. I remember him writing me a brief note to tell me about it. "I guess I'm a part of history now," he said.

There's a photo of twenty-four-year-old Daniel Lawrence Shine in a cool fur-collared bomber jacket. Bill has marked details in the story with a yellow highlighter: ". . . hit with antiaircraft fire over Cologne, Germany. Both Mr. Shine and his bombardier were wounded. Mr. Shine dropped the injured bombardier out the escape hatch before the plane exploded and then experienced a $2\frac{1}{2}$-mile free fall. . . ."

"Is that your father? It doesn't look like him," a nurse says.

Fifty years will do that to you.

To add to his résumé, I explain to the nurse that he has five sons—Danny, Bill, Terry, Chris, and Peter—in that order. Only the three of us have been around the hospital because Peter, the youngest, still lives in New York where we were all raised. I was the first to move to Florida, and in an odd sort of twist on the trickle-down theory, after a few visits Danny made the move and then my parents followed when my father retired. "Everybody wanted to be closer to the sun, not you," Danny always says.

Chris eventually made the pilgrimage to South Florida too but he's the most elusive of the bunch and we haven't even been able to notify him yet.

"Looks like your father was quite a hero," the nurse says, tracing her rubber-gloved finger across the yellow highlights detailing how he was awarded the Purple Heart for his wounds and the Silver Star for his valor.

One rainy day as a kid I was rummaging through boxes in a closet and found a cartoon drawing of our father being blown out of a fat-winged little plane. He explained that when he was in the hospital the people from *Ripley's Believe It or Not* did a sketch of him because they thought it was amazing that he survived. "But they never used it," he said. "I guess they decided it wasn't that amazing after all."

But I thought the idea that my dad was a cartoon was pretty amazing and many a rainy day I would return to that box.

Right now I help make a little collage from some family

photos, but nobody likes it. "It does look stupid," Gerard says.

We argue over where to put photos of him and the grandkids. I want them by his headboard so the army of medical workers taking blood every hour and constantly needling him for tests can see he's not just a gown and limbs. He's a person who stood next to a Christmas tree two weeks ago in a Pebble Beach golf sweater with grandchildren wrapped around his legs. But my brothers think the pictures should be on the far wall—in his line of sight—so they will be immediately visible when he becomes coherent.

They win.

We're not sure but we think he can hear us, so we circle around the bed and exchange stories. Remember the time Dad did this? Remember the time Dad did that?

None of us are great storytellers. Verbally, I am too cryptic to hold an audience. I'm all half sentences and rushing to a conclusion: "Remember when Chris and Pete . . . on the back of the bus . . . yeah, and Dad called Mr. Schiffman— the principal—Mr. Shitman." Bill thinks everything is memorable ("Remember how much you liked making the turkey loaf, Dad?"), and Danny is masterful at getting bogged down in details.

Still, our minds are racing, we're grinding out stories like an eighteen-horsepower wood chipper, filling the room with our shredded memories. I don't know why, but these are mine:

Peter is about five years old. We are all driving home from the Babylon pool when, during a slow wide turn, he rolls out the door of our 1964 Ford Country Squire onto the road. Dad stops, puts Peter back in the car, and we continue on our way. A week later, we are all driving home from the pool when, during a slow wide turn Peter falls out the door onto the road. Dad stops, puts Peter back in the car, and we continue on our way. He is unharmed again but this time my father says we have to start wearing seat belts. "But you don't wear one," Chris says. "As long as I'm holding on to the steering wheel I'm not going to fall into the street," my father says.

"And you never did, did you, Dad?" I laugh into his ear.

It is Saturday. I am ten years old and he has brought us all to work with him. It is a large factory where they make blood-pressure instruments. He is in charge of the accounting and the factory is empty on the weekends so we take the office chairs out to race in the hundred-yard hallways of the plant where me and my brothers find half-used bottles of mercury, spill them out, and play with the silver blobs like they're marbles (maybe that's why we're all a little off). But after the lunch whistle blows our father puts us to work—filing, stuffing envelopes, weighing the mail. And at the end of the day, just as he did all of those Saturdays, he hands us each a pay stub with a black ribbon running across its backside, not unlike the ones we all get today. The amounts vary from week to week—$7.56,

$6.22, $8.78—but we always get our due. We line up in front of a refrigerator-sized safe where he will dip into petty cash. The big silver dial with the red etchings spins in my head. 17 right, 32 left, pass by twice to 24. I can hear the tumblers click and then his hand thrusting down on the shaft.

"Click, click, click . . . I can still hear those tumblers click, Dad. Can you hear them, Dad?"

There is a flagpole in the center of our neighborhood and our family is in charge of raising and lowering the flag on holidays. It must be Columbus or Veterans Day because the air is crisp and I've got a glove on one hand. Night is coming and as I bring it down Chris and I are fighting to see who unhooks it and then both of us are struggling with the cold metal clasps. We are careful that the flag doesn't touch the ground, because that's the rule. We bunch it up in our arms and return to the house where my father calls my other brothers into the room. We line up and stretch the banner the length of our living room as our father guides us through the motions of folding Old Glory military style. Shake it out, half, half again, triangle, step, triangle, step . . . "Tighter, tighter" until no red, no blood is showing. Just the bright blue and the glow of the stars.

"The perfect triangle, Dad. I wonder if we could still do it? The perfect triangle."

We've had our own pool for a few years now, and my parents are throwing a summer party. My brothers and I spend most of the night hiding, peeking through the screens of our bedrooms, listening to the boisterous chatter and clinking of ice. But then there's a sudden silence and spotlights on the pool. I won't get the whole story until later but what's happening is the boyfriend of one of our grown-up cousins, a burly man about ten years younger than my father, has been needling him all night about not going for a swim. My father, being the good host, never swims at his own party but the guy has gone too far, yelling out that my father can't even swim. And now my father has stripped, rested his cocktail on a redwood picnic table and challenged him to race the length of the pool. And there he stands in his boxer shorts, his arms thrust backward, waiting for the shout of Go.

"Go!" and it's all screams and bubbles and . . . and Danny doesn't remember this story. He wasn't there. But how do you convey those vivid pictures in your mind to someone else? Damn it, I want him to be there. But the details that come out of my mouth can't match up to the solid memory—the bullfrog strokes, the blowfish puff of his underwear, the spotlight illuminating the bubbles off his back. I'm trying, I'm trying to make it real for him, but in the end we're really just all left with our own images, aren't we? We really can't truly pry them from one another. A minute ago, when Danny talked about how my father once accidentally pushed a neighbor through the screen on our back porch, I was struggling to be there. *I* missed that one and I want to be able to pop it in my View-Master, hold it up to the light and see Mr. Reynolds reeling backward, my father halfheartedly trying to save the poor fellow until he's enveloped in the fine mesh wiring and slowly tumbling into the thorny bushes below, but I can't. In an odd and gluttonous way, I am envious of everyone's memories now. I want them all.

"So what happened?" Danny says.

"He won. He won!" I say.

"Hey, Dad, remember that one?" Bill says.

Maybe he does, maybe he doesn't. Maybe he can hear us, maybe he can't. No one's able to tell us for sure, so we're coming up with our own answers.

He can hear us. He remembers.

Jim

I spit on the iron and it sizzles.

My shirt collars are all warped and peeling up like old linoleum. I have spent the morning tearing through the closets and throwing half my clothes into black Hefty Leaf bags for Goodwill.

"What are you doing?" my wife, Christine, asks.

"I have to look good," I say.

At work yesterday, riding the elevator to the twelfth floor, a short dark-haired woman began giggling at me.

"You're just like my husband." Her bright red lips parted. "Your shirt, the collar, the . . . Ahhh." She reached up and tried to do a quick alignment but it was useless and she bailed out on the eighth, giggling down the corridor.

We've had a breakdown in communication with hospital personnel this past week and I believe this woman has nailed it for me. It's fashion.

That's what it's come to now. Something tells me that the nurses will start giving us respect; the doctors will start returning our calls; the security guards will stop asking us, "Where are you going?" every time we enter the hospital; the lady in the gift shop will stop following us to see what we're doing behind the rack of Beanie Babies; all of this will happen if we step up our appearance.

We are a motley crew. And the shorts and Pete's Wicked Ale T-shirts and Danny always wearing that stupid fanny pack with his sweatpants are not helping, I've decided. We've been dressing like emergency room people, the family of citizens who cut their heads at barbecues or get in freak car accidents on the way home from the beach and have to show up in flip-flops and half shirts. These poor people are caught with their pants down, but we have no excuse, we have days and days to plan our wardrobe. "We have to start dressing like intensive care people," I tell my wife.

I am certain that the doctors and the nurses will be much more attentive of my father's needs if we only put a little more effort into our appearance. I can a hear a nurse now:

"I know I just checked on Mr. Shine but I'm going to check on him again. Those boys of his are so well-groomed."

Of my four brothers, only Peter has a sense of fashion, but he's in New York and can't save us now. If my mother was up and around in a smart Laura Ashley pantsuit I'm sure the entire staff and several members of the hospital board would be doting on us around the clock, but it is not an option.

Since complications from a hysterectomy in her sixties, she has constantly struggled with her health. She once looked like Lois Lane, but now she is quite frail with short snow-white hair. Like many mothers her age she has become a precious but ornery old lady. She is so distraught that she can't be at the hospital and the helplessness is making her extremely agitated, Bill keeps telling me. We have left Bill with the unenviable job of keeping her abreast of what's going on day to day. He has tried to be honest with her but with our lack of information he's not even sure what the truth is at this point.

"Why don't they teach you this," I say to Christine. "They always talk about how important it is to dress a certain way, cross your legs a certain way for a job interview, but no one talks about what you need to wear to keep your father alive."

So today I am meticulously laying out my best clothes the way Mickey Rourke would before heading to his night manager job at the restaurant in *The Pope of Greenwich Village*, running my thumb and forefinger along the sharp creases of my trousers, spray starching my withered collars.

Did I mention maybe the doctors would start returning my calls if I look sharp?

"Maybe we should get a second opinion?" Bill said yesterday, questioning the diagnosis so far.

"We haven't got a first opinion yet," I told him. "Nobody's talking to us anymore."

Peter has a million questions about the blood thinner Coumadin. He's adamant that the doctors should never have prescribed it for my father's heart condition to begin with. From what he's heard it could have been the cause of the excessive bleeding. "I looked it up on the computer and you can't eat salad when you're on it," he says. "What kind of medication doesn't allow you to eat salad?"

"Dad loved salad," I say.

"I want some answers," he says. "One doctor up here told me he would never prescribe it for his heart patients. He says something as simple as stopping short in your car can cause bleeding in the brain when you're on that stuff. Someone has to give us some answers."

But we keep getting passed up and down the chain of command. No one explained the fact that one doctor becomes the primary on the case and coordinates all procedures until after we'd called a half dozen of the doctors listed on his charts. Not that any of them called us back to tell us that. We had to hear it from a college kid in the snack bar who was recuperating from a street hockey accident. "The primary," he said. "That's the guy you've got to get to."

Once he put us on the right trail, the nurse told us that we had to talk to our father's cardiologist. "But it's his brain that—"

"He's the primary," she said.

But the cardiologist has yet to return our phone calls, not that we're sitting by the phone anyway.

As I head up the walkway to the hospital this morning I'm starting to perspire. I should have worn shorts, but I've decided that rule #27 in our hospital survival guide is: If you expect your father to live and others to keep you abreast of his progress then dress every day as if it is your first job interview after being out of work for eighteen months.

The security guard picks up my scent but he stops short of saying, "Where are you going?" It has been days since we've stopped at the visitors' desk to announce our arrival or pick up a badge. It would be silly. We live here now.

Each night my ICU visitor's badge goes on my nightstand with my keys and wallet. It has become the unexpected essential, an accessory of illness.

Of course, when I get to his room the nurse tells me the doctor was just in. "Which one?" I ask.

"One I haven't seen before," she says.

This is how it works. No matter when you are in the room the doctor has "just been there." You can step out for a soda, you can go to buy a Beanie Baby, you can chase a buffalo nickel that just rolled by the room, you can blank out for a second while trying to recall the last time you ate and *whooosh*—he's in and out.

"You just missed him," the nurse will say.

"But I just stepped out for a—"

"Sorry.

"Oh, he said you can call the office if you really need to talk to him."

Bill comes in and I ask him how I look. "Sharp," he says. "Did you talk to the doctor?"

I'm all dressed up with no doctors to talk to. We're getting aggravated, this incommunicado bit almost seems intentional, as if they're stalling for some reason. We are thinking about threats. We may not know where they live but we know what they drive. We are a fraction of an inch from putting Jell-O in their gas tanks.

We decide the one thing that would probably make us feel better on a day like this would be if we stop respecting doctors. "We won't call them doctor anymore. We'll leave off the title and only call them by their last names," I say. "They hate that."

As the day drags on we reach a point where not calling doctors "doctor" doesn't seem extreme enough. "We should start calling them by their first names, that will get them," Bill says.

But how are we going to find out their first names?

"We'll just call them all Jim," he says.

The Party

The physician who's been the primary on the case, the one who's supposed to coordinate all the others and keep the family up to date, finally phones to tell me he's putting another doctor in charge of my father because, well . . . "I'm not as knowledgeable about the neurological stuff."

He schedules a meeting for this evening. "You'll meet Dr. Bozeki in the conference room near the ICU," he says. "She'll take care of everything from here on out."

I wonder what her first name is?

The conference room turns out to be the nurses' break room, and they're just getting ready to have a platter of neatly rolled cold cuts and a cake for a staffer's birthday.

"All this for us," Danny says.

Dr. Bozeki (not her real name), who looks like an actress playing a doctor—very *ER*—can't be more than twenty-seven, but she still has the power to get a party moved down the hall with a mere, "Please move it."

She asks us to stand around the garbage can by the phone because my brother Pete in New York is being patched in on the speakerphone.

"Hello??" Pete says.

The doctor starts talking quickly. "I didn't know your father. I saw some pictures in there, war hero or whatever . . . but anyway, you have to start thinking about his quality of life from this point on. Did your father ever . . ."

Oh, I get the doctor switch now. That "I'm not as knowledgeable about the neurological stuff" translates to: Let's bring in a young doctor and give her the shit job of telling the family that it's the end of the line. She needs the experience anyway.

"Did your father ever talk about death with any of you? Did the subject come up in conversation?" she says, each of the questions landing with a thud, like mangoes from a tree.

We are not yet aware that the subject will come up in every conversation we have from this point on but right now it seems too soon. We are in shock.

"You still there, Peter?" the doctor asks.

Peter's still there.

All our days till now have been spent waiting for the swelling to go down so we'll have him back, at least long enough to finish that sentence.

"You have to understand no one has been telling us honestly what's going on with our father," I say. "Up to this point, no one has said how bad it is. They say we just have to wait and see. Are we seeing now?"

"It's not that people aren't being honest with you," she replies. "It's just that with this kind of condition, we can only tell how he's doing by what kind of progress he makes."

And he's not making any. She doesn't need to tell us that.

But we know he's still in there. We've seen glimpses of the real him in the squeeze of a hand, a hint of expression, a fleeting moment of eye contact.

"The nurses aren't seeing those things," Dr. Bozeki says.

A couple of nurses boisterously fling open the door and then go speechless as they gaze upon us all standing around the garbage can talking about death.

"The party moved," I say.

"Anyway," the doctor continues, "it's time for you to decide this: If your father's heart stops, do we restart it? The consensus of all his doctors is not to."

Our consensus is *to.*

The doctor also has one of my father's nurses on hand (a good one) for support and she asks her to step forward.

"You shouldn't restart it," the nurse says.

She steps backward.

We don't know what to say. Up until now the biggest decision most of us have made in our lives is whether to buy or lease.

Our minds are reeling. How did we go from waiting for the plateau to pulling plugs in only a matter of days?

"How much recovery time is a person allowed?" I ask.

"It depends," she answers.

"Would not restarting his heart include withholding suste-nance and water?" Bill says.

"Has your father talked to you about this?" Bozeki asks pointedly.

Bill says, "Yeah," but doesn't give her any more detail.

He wants to know more about how much progress they actually think my father can make. "Would he be able to watch TV?" he asks.

"There's more to life than watching TV," the doctor says.

We all look at one another.

It is times like this when I know my brothers and I are truly related and God, I wish I had a sister.

"So, you're saying he'll be able to watch TV?" Danny says.

The doctor sees she's getting nowhere, tells us to sleep on it, and quickly exits. Probably in a hurry to get to the party.

"Peter, are you still there?" the nurse asks.

Peter's still there.

"OK, we're going to hang up on you now," the nurse says.

"OK," Peter says.

Dad's Wishes

We're in the hospital snack bar, two minutes away from our garbage-can meeting.

"They have the best two-fifty ham and cheese sandwiches here," Danny says, rubbing his hands together. "I could go for one right now."

We decide to have Colombo frozen yogurt and sit down in one of the green and purple *Happy Days* booths.

"He has a living will, you know," Bill says nonchalantly, staring down at the black-and-white checkered tabletop.

So that was where that hydration and sus-te-nance talk was coming from.

"Dad really did talk to you about death, didn't he?" I say. We're all jealous. He never talked to me about death. "Danny, did he ever talk to you about death?"

"Nope."

Why didn't you tell the doctor?

He has no answer other than the obvious. "What if they look at it and just start pulling all the plugs?"

So begins a game of hide-and-seek with the living will. The next morning I call the doctor's office and tell the receptionist there's a living will so at least it's out in the open. I'm just going to get a copy from Bill and give it to the doctor.

"I think we should take it to a lawyer," Bill says.

"Why? That's silly. He went to a lawyer to have the damn thing written up," I say.

It's Dad's wishes. Even if we don't want to give it to them, it's not up to us, I convince myself. I'm just going to hand it over. I'm not even going to look at it.

I look at it.

It's all jargon, and what I can make out doesn't look good.

TO MY FAMILY, MY PHYSICIAN, MY ATTORNEY, MY
CLERGYMAN: TO ANY FACILITY IN WHOSE CARE
I HAPPEN TO BE: TO ANY INDIVIDUAL WHO MAY
BECOME RESPONSIBLE FOR MY HEALTH, WEL-
FARE OR AFFAIRS:

THIS DECLARATION, made the 11th day of May,
1992, I being of sound mind, willfully and volun-
tarily make known my desire that my dying shall
not be artificially prolonged under the circumstances set forth below, do hereby declare:

IF AT ANY TIME, I should have an incurable injury,
disease or illness regarded as a terminal condition
by my physician, and if my physician has deter-
mined that the application of life-sustaining procedures would serve only to artificially prolong the
dying process and that my death will occur whether
or not life-sustaining procedures are utilized, I
direct that such procedures, including the intuba-
tion for sustenance and hydration, be withheld or
withdrawn and that I be permitted to die with only
the administration of medication or the perfor-
mance of any medical procedure deemed necessary
to provide me with comfort care, with the excep-
tion of providing for sustenance and hydration.

IN THE ABSENCE of my ability to give directions
regarding the use of such life-sustaining procedures, it is my intention that this Declaration shall

be honored by my family and physician as the final expression of my legal right to refuse medical or surgical treatment and accept the consequences from such refusal, and that I have discussed my views as to life-sustaining measures with my friends and family, all of whom understand my wishes.

I UNDERSTAND the full import of this Declaration, and I am emotionally and mentally competent to make this declaration.

Daniel L. Shine

I try to grasp what I can. Is this considered an injury, an illness, a disease? I guess it's a "condition," but is it a "terminal condition"? Nobody has declared that with any certainty. "He could surprise us," is still a constant refrain. So much so, that I wonder if it's only another way of saying: "Hey, stupid, your father is dying but I'm not going to be the one to tell you." But there's only so much I can assume or wonder about. And what about the part where it says "my death will occur whether or not life-sustaining procedures are utilized"? That is not true, is it? No doctors are saying they're sustaining him for no reason. At least not yet. At least not until they get this piece of paper, I bet.

It looks as if it came right down to it, he'd rather just be starved to death if it means having to be on any machines at all. Right now he's being fed through tubes and he's on a ventilator, not breathing on his own. Does this paper mean they would cut off his air?

And another question keeps nagging me: If he's so set on abiding by the guidelines of a living will, why didn't he bring it with him when he checked into the hospital for brain surgery? Why wasn't it right there on his chart from the very beginning?

But as soon as I think that, I can hear him say, "Terry, I'm not gonna jinx it. You don't show up with a living will when you're going to be coming home on Friday."

I keep reading it over and over but then I realize, if I've read it a dozen times, knowing my father, he read it a thousand times before signing it. He knew what he was doing. Oh, Dad, it's us. *We* don't know what we're doing.

Circling the Drain

Dad has a mustache.

He's never had one before in his life but now, here in ICU room number sixteen where the days grow like hair, he's got a mustache.

"I can never get mine to come in that full," I say.

Danny likes it, at first. "But there must be a reason he never had a mustache," he says. "Do you think we should say something?"

We should, but with all the complications we decide it can wait.

"You're his sons, aren't you?"

I turn and one of the nurses who was at the Do Not Resuscitate meeting but didn't step forward has stationed herself in one corner of the room, behind a series of monitors. She is stout and gray, standing staunchly with her arms folded, a pillar of hard-hearted cynicism.

"If you want to see an example of what could happen to your father if his heart stops and we have to restart it, go check out bed number fourteen," she says to us. "That guy's circling the drain."

I flinch, she doesn't. She continues to hang around the room like the Grim Reaper, trying to convince us to sign the Do Not Resuscitate order. Now she's got us thinking that, at the very least, our father could become next month's prime example. *"Check out bed number sixteen."*

We know it doesn't work the way it does on *ER* (because we asked—"Doesn't it work like on *ER*?"). We know people don't get jolted back three or four times and just take it in stride, reach over to the Dean Koontz novel they've got spread open to pages 212 and 213 on the food tray, and say, "Now, where was I?"

We are not completely delusional. We know even if someone gets a hearty beep back on the monitor he still may never know where he is.

When the nurse walks away Danny asks me if I think we could sign something that instead of having big block lettering that says DO NOT RESTART THIS MAN'S HEART UNDER ANY CIRCUMSTANCES, could say something more like: AT LEAST TRY ONCE.

Bring him back from the dead once, that seems like a fair compromise. Maybe we are completely delusional.

When the heart shuts down it's the body's way of saying it's time to die, Bozeki has told us. "It's that simple."

It makes sense, but not to us.

We were raised on the brain-dead theory; that's when you give it all up. When the doctor pulls you aside and says, "I'm sorry, your father is brain-dead." When he walks you over to that brain-wave machine and all you see is a line as clean and straight as a master carpenter's markings on a two-by-four, and he says: "There's nothing more we can do." *That's* when you give up. Not when they herd you around a garbage can and tell you: Well, he's an old guy and maybe he'll be able to watch TV again some day, who knows.

Nobody knows, that's the thing, and they tell you that point-blank just before they hand you the pen.

His lips are so dry. They have this strawlike thing with Styrofoam at the end that I asked about one day, and the nurse told me it could be used to swab the mouth. "Do *you* want to do it?" he said, like, *don't be thinking I've got the time to be messin' with that*.

"Yes, I do," I said.

And each day since I dab cold water on the blue spongy end and run it over his tongue and gums. With the first drop of moisture his back arches up like a parched man lying in the desert who suddenly feels a drop of rain. But then he settles down and seems to find it soothing, as do I.

Danny can't stop thinking about what's going on in my father's mind. The doctors keep taking CAT scans, but they say they can't tell if he's having mini-strokes in there or what. "Nothing shows up." They shrug.

Danny's questions have become abstract. If he sees us, does he know who we are, and if things are so jumbled up does he envision us as we are today, or does he hear the voices of his children from forty years ago? Is it like being in a fever, one hallucination piling up on the next? Is it circuits breaking and a series of frazzled eclipses, windows to reality that only last a fraction of a second?

"What's going on in there?" Danny says, tightening his fists.

Another nurse comes in, looks at my father's chart for a minute and says, "You should really think about taking him home. One of you needs to quit your job and take care of him full time."

This is why all decisions are frozen, I realize. It's like everyone in the hospital is taking orders from some Jabberwock who erratically and spontaneously spits out instructions. "Oh, if they don't go for the not starting the heart thing direct them to Mr. Circling the Drain and if that doesn't close the deal just tell them to quit their jobs, take him home and feed him plenty of soup. Soup, soup, soup."

Later I will call Dr. Bozeki on this one and she will say: "*Take him home?* Oh, no, you can't listen to the nurses."

Well, who the hell are we supposed to listen to?

"I would like to quit my job," Danny says, pondering what the nurse had said.

I continue to marvel at Danny's hospital persona. There seems to be a closeness between my father and him that I had never perceived before. Pushing fifty, almost ten years older than the rest of us, he had my father all to himself for so many years. But by the time I was old enough to collect memories he was a teenager and there was a lot of tension between the two of them. I'd listen to them argue and then stare and giggle at Danny as he came out to watch TV with us and make wisecracks about Efrem Zimbalist Jr. and other characters on the shows. "What are you lookin' at?" he'd say, making me squirm.

His teenage world provided so much entertainment for us. When he was about seventeen he actually turned our basement into some kind of teen nightclub. He called it the Polaris Inn, even had business cards made up at the print shop at school. He hung different colored sheets from the pipes and beams to turn the open basement into separate rooms—one for shooting pool, one for doing shots of swiped Early Times bourbon, one for making out, I imagined. And every weekend the music would blast and tangerine-smelling girls would be lined up our basement steps, the phone cord from the kitchen stretching down the stairway. I would have to get in line behind strangers to use my own bathroom. And when it was time to go to bed I would sometimes lay my blanket on the ground, put my ear to the floor, and fall asleep listening to the crazy sounds of his life.

He lives so quietly now, his wisecracks aged to a mellow goofiness. He has a job at Sears, lives in a sparsely populated neighborhood in St. Lucie County in a house with no basement, and he rarely makes me squirm anymore. As he grips my father's hand in the way only men do, locked and loaded in an inexplicable bond, I know it is the most sincere thing I will ever witness.

Danny's a single parent and his eleven-year-old son goes everywhere with him, including hospitals. He's not allowed in the ICU so I always run into him out in the corridors and empty my pockets of change since—like father, like son—the highlights of his hospital visits always center around the vending machines.

At the moment, Danny and I are thirsty and thinking about joining him for a Dr Pepper but we're trying to figure a way to get out without getting pulled into the downward spiral of bed number fourteen. "I don't want to pass by there," I say. "I don't want my eyes to be drawn to whatever that Grim Reaper wants us to see."

"We've been here so much I think we can make it out with our eyes closed," Danny says.

Before exiting the room, I look back at the mustache. It's just sitting there on his face . . . waiting.

Surprise

His legs are kicking and his arms are flailing and this is no seizure.

After the doomsday talk from Bozeki, while the rest of us were whining, Bill had spent hours with Dad, barking directly into his ear. Telling him he had to put on a show or the doctors were going to give up on him.

And something must have clicked because today he's dancing. We brought in some of his CDs. Louis and Ella are on the boom box and his toe is tappin'.

We are impressed.

But the nurses aren't. They look at us like, "*Yeah, that's OK if you want someone who's just going to tap his toe for the rest of his life.*"

They want to see more than instinctive movement and the following of commands. They want to see communication.

"Dad, can you respond to a question by holding up one finger for yes and two for no?" Bill says.

Nothing.

But we keep working, trying different things.

I tickle his feet, but Danny scolds me. "You don't tickle a man when he's in this condition."

New family rule: We're to do everything in our power to bring him back around, but we draw the line at tickling.

My elusive brother Chris has come to the hospital for the first time and my father seems to jolt at the sound of his voice. His body lunges forward as if to say, "Chris, where have you been?"

"Dad, it's me, Chris," he says.

Chris is lean and tall and has an Abe Lincoln–without–the–beard appearance. As kids he was always the one who took the reins of a situation. If we were all at the Sizzler on Montauk Highway and suddenly realized there was no ketchup on the table, Chris, even when he was only ten, was the one who would get up, find the person in charge, point across the dining area and say, "You see that family over there? They have no ketchup." But in adulthood we've had to fend for ourselves because he's become aloof and doesn't keep us abreast of what he's up to.

His voice is gentle and he slowly steps around to the opposite side of the bed. He lowers his head and whispers in my father's other ear. "Dad, it's me, Chris."

He moves in closer until his head is almost resting on the pillow next to my father's right ear and continues the mantra: "Dad, it's me, Chris."

The pulmonary doctor, a young guy who looks sort of like a QVC fitness guru, charges in and gives us a little pep talk, tells us to keep it up. "Don't worry about what the nurses think. He responds to you guys. You gotta keep working it," he says, fiddling with the end of his stethoscope as if any second he's going to put it to his lips, blow it like a whistle, and my father is going to shoot out of the starting blocks. "Before you know it he'll be ready for aggressive rehab. Just keep it up, up, up. You are making a difference."

As soon as he leaves the room, Bill says: "Mitsubishi 3000 GT. Black."

I mention to one of the nurses that we really like that doctor, and she explains to me in her own convoluted way that the personable doctors are the bad doctors and the ones with no personality are the ones you'd actually want operating on you. "Well, in that case, I think we've got some of the best on this case," I say.

Our brother Peter bursts into the room. There is no door to swing open or even a curtain to throw aside but he always oozes adrenaline and his stocky Baretta build pushes you aside. He's come directly from the airport and he's desperately charged up. "Dad, it's me, Pete. Nod if you can hear me."

He nods.

We jump in the air. How could we not think of the nod? How come you didn't think of the nod, I punch Danny. Why do we have to fly a guy in from New York to come up with the nod?

"Shouldn't the doctors have thought of the nod?" Danny says.

Believe me, we're not high-five people, but we're high-fiving. For me, it's a first. "You're not good at it," Danny says.

I've got a copy of the living will in my pocket, but

there's no need for it now. If they want to know if he wants his heart restarted they can ask him.

We've got his attention.

"If anyone can pull through this, you can, Dad," Bill says.

We run into the hallway and drag a nurse in. "Ask him a question," Peter demands. She asks. He nods yes. He shakes no.

"So, what are you going to tell the doctors if they ask if he's able to communicate?" Peter corners her. "What are you going to say?"

She nods yes.

Yes, victory. We have communication, we have confirmation. We have . . . progress.

We're progress in motion. We've got all four corners of his bed covered. We don't know how long this window of coherency is going to last so we're frantically asking yes and no questions and manipulating his arms and legs.

He's shuffling his legs around like he's restless and he wants to get up and walk. I take my hands and apply pressure to the soles of his feet and he starts pumping his legs. His knees are up and he's wildly pedaling against my hands.

"Yeah, this is OK if you want someone who's just going to ride a bike around for the rest of his life," I howl.

A prim elderly woman in a fancy pantsuit and large handbag passes by the door and gloomily smiles at us like she does every time she's here visiting her husband down the hall. But this time she sees our father in action, backs up, leans in the doorway, pumps her fist like Pat Riley, and says, "Yes!"

I ask him for the thumbs-up. He delivers. Applause breaks out. The nurse catches the erect thumb out of the corner of her eye and gives us a sort of pitiful grin. *"Yeah, that's OK, if you want someone who's just going to give you the thumbs-up for the rest of his life."*

She's the rain pouring through our open window, but we're not going to let her bring it all down. Louis and Ella are singing, "Let it snow, let it snow . . ." and even Gerard is dancing.

The blue eyes are clear.

"I love you, Dad," Pete says.

"I can't believe we didn't think of the nod," Danny says.

The Daily News

We're coming from opposite ends of the hospital parking lot. We've got newspapers tucked under our arms.

We both have big plans today. I'm going to turn that corner to the hospital room and Dad's going to be feeling good enough to sit up and I'm going to read him current events—the prime is down and John Glenn is going back up.

Bill has bigger plans. "I brought his reading glasses," he says. "So he can read the paper himself."

We are only a couple of days from the thumbs-up, but he's a million miles away. There will be no reaching him today. For the first time, I not only feel sorry for my father but I feel sorry for us.

We are standing on opposite sides of the bed, our papers in hand, and we do look pitiful. Is this what the nurses have been seeing?

My father lying there motionless. Us, incessantly, relentlessly trying to get a rise, a trick out of him like he's a show pony, when maybe all he needs is some peace.

I wonder if our one great day with Louis and Ella wasn't quite the glorious lift toward the plateau we'd been hoping for but more of a gift, a chance for us to openly profess our love and for him to give us the nod of acceptance.

I notice one of the neurosurgeons shoot by the room and give chase. I ask him if he can really tell me where we're at. "Think of it like the spinning plates of a circus performer," he says. "With your dad, one plate is his hypertension, one is his heart condition, one is his age, one is bleeding on both sides of the brain."

"Thanks," I say.

"Where we at?" Bill says when I get back to the room.

"We're spinning plates," I say.

A wide-eyed nurse with long dark hair whom we haven't seen before comes into the room and asks if we are his sons.

"This is Terry and I'm Will," Bill introduces us.

"I've heard about you guys," she says. "I know your father can hear what you're saying. He changes when you're in the room."

She leaves the room and we can't think of a thing to say, a thing to change him.

They did mention he may be getting out of ICU soon, saying he's getting slightly stronger physically, if not mentally.

You know, when he was responding with hand signals and whatnot I had asked Bozeki if we could hold up the living will and ask him for a yes or no, and she said absolutely not. I scoffed at her at the time but I realize now how important the words "emotionally and mentally competent" were before he put his signature on that document. Any man at this point, lying there clamped down like a trapped animal with burning medicine chasing the pain through his veins, is going to want to desperately fight it to the end. Just as they say the soul is the last thing to leave the body, mental competence must be the first thing to flee in a situation such as this. Not only for him, but for all of us, I am afraid. Like a crazed animal, at this point the only thing his body has left to offer is instinct and insanity. And it's become so hard to trust our judgment because I wonder if we are not on the same course.

I think about how when I talked to Pete last night he said, "Well, all we can do is keep praying," and I conveniently agreed. But I do not pray, I only wait.

We were all raised Catholic, spent the early years in neighbors' basements where the moms took on the responsibility of teaching catechism. At the end of class at Mrs. Mavis's house, I would always walk around the Ping-Pong table to a crucifix that rested on a wool blanket atop her dryer. She would hold it up for each of us to kiss the tiny feet—purse our lips around the porcelain toes and buy a ticket up the stairs to the rest of the day.

We had tests every week—multiple choice, true and false, fill in the blank. I got an "A" in catechism and thought, I'm smart in religion. Now, I have no idea what I was thinking because I can't seem to summon up so much as a shot glass full of spirituality to help me through this. I can't remember a single answer.

I look at Bill and wonder why we haven't seen each other in so long. For years he had crisscrossed the country nonstop, hauling cargo for several trucking companies, but he's been settled here lately and still we don't get together.

When I was a kid I used to snicker when I heard an uncle or someone say, "Oh, I haven't seen my brother Tim in seven years." What's that all about? I thought. How the heck could you go years without seeing your brother?

Brotherhood ends. I would have thought that a fat lie.

But here I stand. Are we at that point in life where the only things that will bring us together are death and illness? We're all too busy for one another. We're all too busy doing nothing.

I guess the distance from Bill began when he joined the

air force in the early seventies. Until then he was the typical older brother—bigger, stronger, smarter. When Danny moved out of the house all my focus turned to Bill. I remember sitting in the kitchen while he was in the basement pounding on a speed bag rigged to the ceiling. The whole house would shake. Someday he'd teach me how to make the whole house shake, I figured. But then he disappeared.

And that's when the elephants started coming. I guess I was around fourteen, and he had been stationed in Thailand for about two months during the tail end of the Vietnam War when the elephants began arriving at our house in a parade of UPS trucks. There were elephant bookends, elephant lamps and tables, and there were elephants that just stood in the living room basking in the sun. These weren't silly circus elephants. These were serious elephants.

They were the type of elephants you'd find holding down the rug in one of those fancy gift shops that people walk through looking at prices and then just buy a key chain. Each one was given a territory on a whim, from one end of our house to the other. They stalked the dust by day and my dreams by night. They had traveled so far and I couldn't understand why.

I wrote Bill dozens of letters and between letting him know our dog, an Airedale named Sean, was eating nothing but spaghetti for dinner and how we'd finally laid sod in the backyard, I would question him about the elephants, making him aware of my intrigue. "What's going on? Why are you sending them in herds?"

He never wrote back but the elephants kept coming. I began cursing the sight of them. I knew other guy's brothers were overseas getting great deals on 35mm cameras and stereo systems. I'd seen speakers the size of refrigerators. I could only pray we wouldn't get an elephant the size of a refrigerator. I wouldn't be able to sleep.

I imagined there must have been a beautiful Asian girl in the village and the only way to her heart was by purchasing the elephants her father worked on into the night. Or maybe they were a newfound religious symbol to him. They were Buddhas with trunks and somewhat fatter asses. He was going to come home and take them door to door, spreading the word.

It seems now that the more I daydreamed about the elephants the less I feared what being in Southeast Asia on the fringe of a war might do to him.

When the elephants stopped arriving I knew my brother was coming home. We all went to greet him. I was going to get my brother back, but as we waited in the airport he passed right by all of us. I didn't know who he was. He seemed a foot shorter, meatless, wiry in a distorted way. Different.

But shortly after, he came back into focus. The meat was returning to his bones, he bought a black Plymouth hemi-Cuda with a straight-line shifter, and the house was starting to shake again. I never even asked him about the elephants.

It didn't seem to matter now that he was home. But then Bill was transferred to a military base in New Hampshire, the land of the big lakes, and I was left with nothing but little brothers.

"What's with the 'Will'?" I say, breaking the silence.

I'd been letting it slide. I'd noticed that he kept referring to himself as Will now. One day I came in and the nurse said, "Oh, Will was just here," and I had to think for a second whom she meant. He's always been Bill.

"We're going through enough right now without you throwing a name change into the mix. You can't just switch like that," I say. "It's not like a split personality thing or your new Muslim name, is it? . . . Because if it is your new Muslim name, let me tell you, it's much too short."

"It's just new." He smiles.

Getting Our Wires Crossed

I am alone today.

It is only my father and me and the blip blips of this submarine existence of stainless steel fixtures and monitors tracking the course.

They have moved him out of intensive care because his vital signs have stabilized to a certain degree. "He's graduating!" was the way Bozeki put it. "He's making a step up."

He made this step before, after the initial surgery, and

that's when everything went haywire. I am desperate for something positive to happen, but my cynicism makes me wonder if our graduation celebration is due to the fact that they needed to open up a bed in ICU for someone else—someone younger, someone stronger, someone with a future.

His hands are fastened down, but struggling frantically, so I set them free, and they start roaming across his chest. I intertwine his fingers with mine and raise his hands over his head—up and down, up and down. He winces, he grimaces, he leads the way for a moment, and then his arms collapse and his hands dig beneath the hospital gown.

Lights start flashing, a beep turns into an alarm.

Panicked, I look at the screens on the several aluminum totem poles surrounding him but I can't tell what's what. He is haphazardly wired like an old British Leyland sports car. He must have pulled off one of the connectors is all.

I begin digging around in the folds of the linen but his hands get in the way. The thought of setting them free was much easier than the idea of having to tie down your own father's limbs, a gesture that can only increase his suffering.

I let his fingers roam but squeeze behind his bed to see where everything is leading. The confusion and claustrophobia in the tight space is similar to the feeling I get every time I step behind a stereo system. I wish Chris were here, he's good with mechanical stuff.

This is how the majority of the days drag on now for my brothers and me. One of us is here, one of us is gone. We cross paths, change shifts, leave notes. When I'm alone I am less apt to try and capture my father's attention. I sit quietly in a chair, meditating, as if I'm in a church during midweek when the pews are empty and the stillness eerie. They call it "holding vigil," I guess, but it makes me feel useless. When nurses tread by I try to talk them up to see where we're at, and they always want to step outside the room because you're not supposed to talk about the patient as if he's not there. "Then talk about him like he's here. Tell him, instead of me," I say. I force the issue and they make an honest effort, their eyes jumping from me to my father, not sure where their allegiance lies anymore.

But sometimes I take that walk into the hall so he doesn't have to hear the same news over and over and sometimes I keep walking until I'm outside, standing in the crisp air, because maybe I get tired of *thinking* about him in front of him, I don't know.

There is a meditation room at the hospital and a court-yard where the statue of a Franciscan monk stands in the corner barefoot, a bird perched on his shoulder, but I prefer to stand in the east parking lot and watch mothers head home with their new babies, pink or blue balloons attached to their wheelchairs, dads pulling up in minivans. I see peo-ple going into the billing offices with envelopes and papers in hand, shaking their heads when they go in, shaking them harder when they come out. The doctors' parking lot is up front, this is where Will must do his spying. It is here on this strip of concrete that extends out like a pier across the lot that on another day I run head-on into the brain doctor, who, the night before, had probed inside my father's head and then sat six inches from my face telling the Jell-O story. When we walk toward each other in broad daylight less than twelve hours later he does not acknowledge me, nor I him, for that matter.

Since I stand outside as if I'm killing time, idling in the afternoon breeze, people will ask me for a cigarette, or if I've got a light. "I am not on a cigarette break," I say.

I often walk out to the edge of the concrete pier and stop as if I can go no farther, as if I am truly trapped here. My feet dangle over the edge and I let everything swirl around me.

It is oddly chilly today so I step out from the shade of the building's rounded awnings in search of some warmth. There is no comfort I know that is better than that patch of sun you find on an unexpectedly cold day. I still find that place easy to wallow in. While standing in a small island of light, the heat lowering the goose bumps on my arms, I daydream of what it would be like if my father suddenly began to recover. If, while sitting back in that room reading *Newsweek*'s conventional wisdom chart or counting the nurses passing by the door, a voice suddenly cracked the monotony: "Terry, it's me, your father."

"Dad??"

From those words would come a string of soft afternoons on the way to his complete recovery, hours of sitting at his side talking about medical mishaps, fists flying during another Knicks-Heat game, grandchildren, golf swings, and what day it is today and what day it was yesterday and what day it will be tomorrow. The back of the bed is propped, he is fragile but trying to chomp on a hospital cut of sirloin. It's medium-rare.

"Where is my checkbook?"

"Terry, shouldn't you be at work?"

Those questions would come, I'm sure. And on some Saturday all of our paths would cross, each of my brothers would stand at the corners of his bed once again, only this time our father would be the live wire in the center of it all, somehow pulling us all closer together.

I get back to the room and reality is a young woman with stringy brown hair sitting there, reading my magazine. She is from an outside nursing service and has been hired to monitor my father's breathing since they took him off the respirator.

After our show of my father's bicycle-riding abilities that one day and other tests, the pulmonary doctor decided he was progressing enough to be removed from the ventilator. But the act of breathing becomes the biggest strain at this point and some of the family has feared that just as his mind is improving, his lungs will fail him and since we're out of intensive care the attention of the hospital staff is no longer at maximum. So we have hired an LPN who does nothing but listen to his breathing and read my magazines. The insurance does not cover it, and at twenty-four hours a day, it will cost over a thousand dollars a week. I, myself, have argued that our desperation is going to overwhelm us and that this is the first sign.

"But if this is it, we've got to give him every chance," Peter says. "We can't let him slip away because some nurse doesn't happen to check on him in time. This way we have no doubt."

But there are still so many doubts.

We're covering *ourselves* now, I'm beginning to understand that.

I'm also beginning to understand that just as my father must see each of his sons differently, each of his sons sees a different father. I can hear it in the stories we tell. In Danny's, who is the eldest, he's a no-nonsense tough guy who can be a bit fallible; in Peter's, who is the baby, he's a hero figure who can do no wrong; in mine, the middle child, he is an everyman whose sensibilities somehow hoist him above average. And when it comes to medical decisions like the breathing situation I can see how to some of us he is Dad, a stoic figure of stability, but to others he is still Daddy and he dare not leave us when we still need him so much. With each decision, I wonder, is he counting on us, or are we counting on him?

Nancy, an extremely caring nurse, pokes her head in and says, "Is everything OK?" and stays around long enough to wait for an answer. When several of the nurses got an attitude about us hiring our own nurse, as if we were trying to insult them, Nancy came to the rescue and advised us that no extra precautions we take at this point could ever be considered wrong.

It is the one rule we will not forget.

Since I'm in the room, I suppose, our new private-duty nurse gets up and adjusts the breathing tube in his trachea and then sits back down. I take a seat in the chair at the opposite side of the room, and we both just listen to my father's breathing.

Inhale . . . exhale . . . inhale . . . exhale . . . . inhale . . . exhale. I try to follow it to see if there's a pattern I can attach myself to. I close my eyes and listen to the erratic rhythm. Inhale . . . exhale . . . . inhale . . .

When I open my eyes Danny and Will are in the room. Danny's got some news. First: "Has anyone seen my Chieftains CD? The nursing supervisor said she had everyone looking for it but it was nowhere to be found. I think I know who took it."

"Who?" I ask.

"I don't want to say until I'm sure," he says.

Second: He's been talking on the phone to our cousin Jill all afternoon.

Jill?

I haven't seen her since I was three feet high. Her mom, Betty, is one of the aunts I was talking about who have such an impact on your world when you're a child but then disappear from your life once everybody stops getting together for Christmas and you stop hearing her smoky singing voice and seeing her banging on the piano pedals with her gold slippers. When my aunt Betty died a decade ago I sent a note to Jill at her home in Cold Spring Harbor but it was more about support than my own sense of loss. I knew something great was gone but I could not feel it.

The same problem relates to cousins, I guess. Unless someone really makes an effort, those fringe relationships just crumble.

Jill? Geeze, what's she doing these days?

Other than being a fifty-year-old woman now, she's a college teacher in Miami, only about ninety minutes away.

"She's on her way here," Danny says. "She's coming to visit at five-thirty."

Her one brother and father are also deceased, and I realize we are her closest living relatives. Of course she is coming. We have a big sister now. Someone who will add wisdom and make sense of all this.

"As long as you all are here, I'm going to step out and get an iced tea," our costly nurse says.

I look around. Even without the equipment, it is once again getting pretty crowded in here.

"I was just in the gift shop. They have the biggest bags of Goldfish I've ever seen," Danny mentions. "Ten times the size of the ones you see in the grocery stores."

I am not alone.

The Next Question . . .
Could Be Your Last

It's 4:30 A.M. and the beeper that's in the pocket of my pants, crumpled in the middle of the bedroom floor, is letting loose with a scary shrill.

The number is unrecognizable, but that's nothing new. I make the call and give a groggy hello. It's Dr. Bozeki and she sounds as if she's been up for hours.

She has. There have been some severe complications. Dad's blood pressure went way down and they barely got him back. She wants another meeting. And you might want to bring that living will you've been hiding, she says in a knowing and motherly tone. *It's time for you boys to stop playing games.*

Along with the beeper comes the honor of being family spokesman. I have to make the tedious calls to each of my brothers and explain the situation. They immediately have questions to which I have no answers. "You should have asked the doctor that." Yeah, I know, I should have asked the doctor that. I try to write down questions to ask, but I never ask enough because doctors are masterful at making your next question the last. Having them actually return my phone calls is much worse than when they were ignoring us. It's like, "OK, your father is dying and I'm the appointed primary on the case but don't be calling me all the time and asking these annoying questions."

Every conversation goes like this:

"Doctor, the nurse said you can't give him the Coumadin to stop the clots?"

"That's right, it's a catch-22. He needs the thinner to stop the strokes but the thinner will make his brain bleed out, so I will keep you up to date."

"Wait, I have another question. If we take him off the ventilator, can he breathe on his own?"

"We can't be positive, but the respiratory therapists feel that he wouldn't have a problem, so I will keep you up to date."

"Wait, I have another . . ."

Click.

"Did the doctor hang up on you?" my wife asks.

I'm not sure. They're so masterful at it. I wasn't done, but she was, so maybe that's not considered hanging up. I'm just not sure.

In the wee hours of this morning, the only call I don't mind making is to Will because I like to say his new name and let him know I'm on board with it. I'm down with the new name. "Will, it's Terry."

But he gets on my nerves when he begins to tell me that he can't accept this. "You don't know," he says, "how hard this is on me."

And I want to scream. *Hard on you*, what about me? As if he's not my father, too. You cannot come to me for comfort.

But I know he's spent. He's been living with my mother, so he's got the job of walking her through it day by day. One day he's got good news, the next worse, the next bad, the next better. It's a bizarre roller coaster.

I realize for the first time that despite all the twists and curves and ups and downs, there is only one thing that's going to get us off this dizzying ride.

Death.

What It Takes

I've got the living will in my back pocket and I'm counting the doctor's minutes until Dr. Bozeki arrives. She said she'd meet us in our father's room.

Not that it's even him in it anymore. There's this guy lying there who's fighting the fetal position, his mouth hanging open like a sleeping dog, arms purple from being poked and prodded for weeks. His skin is elastic; his arms are still tied down so he won't accidentally *or intentionally* pull the oxygen tube from his trachea and he still has that mustache.

"They shaved the rest of his face. Why do they keep leaving that?" Bill asks.

Not that it doesn't look good on him.

"It's really gotten bushy. Very aristocratic," Danny says.

It seems so odd though, the man never even had a five o'clock shadow and now he looks like one of the British commanders in the movie *Zulu*. We really should say something.

"I'm not going to, but you should," Will says. "You're the family spokesman."

But again, we decide it can wait.

"Hey, Terry, did you go back to sleep this morning?" A happy voice pops up behind me. It's our actress doctor.

She is so beautiful. Asian American, skin that holds up even in hospital light, catalog clothes, and heels that lift her to meet our eyes. What a great angel she'd make but she's just our doctor, flipping the charts and giving us a few vital moments of her time, just another doctor.

"What?" I say, irritated by her cheeriness.

"Were you able to go back to sleep after I called?"

"No, I went for a run," I say.

"Me, too," she says, ending with the only thing we have in common.

I pull the living will out of my pocket and hand it to her. Will sees me out of the corner of his eye but doesn't say anything.

We've done nothing but go back and forth on it. Ending but not ending at all with the fact that it doesn't belong to us. Dad only told us where it was. We have no right to hide it, we decided, but still we did nothing but stare at it.

Bozeki begins reading it immediately and then walks me out to a phone by the nurses' station. She's got the spinning-plates neurosurgeon on the line. "He wanted to be at the meeting but he got tied up, so he wants to talk to you on the phone," she says, handing me the receiver.

This is not good. He starts off with the last thing a family wants to hear at a time like this. "Terry, your father just doesn't have what it takes. Other people could have come through this, but not him."

What the . . . ? Where's the lead-up? Terry, your father is one tough son of a gun and he's given it a hell of a fight, but this is just too much. He's in a hole that no one could get out of . . .

Just doesn't have what it takes. I thank God I'm the only one hearing this. It would break my brothers' hearts. *If anyone can pull through this, you can, Dad.*

And he's just getting started. I don't know if he thinks I'm a simpleton, or if perhaps when you're a brain surgeon everyone is a simpleton, but he starts bombarding me with inane metaphors.

"Let's put it this way, Terry. If a friend from across town called to tell you he was coming by your house tomorrow and then twenty-five days went by and he still hadn't shown up, what would you think?"

I'd think he'd decided not to bother coming over.

"OK, how 'bout this. What if you were at a candy vending machine and put a quarter in for an item but it doesn't come out. How many quarters are you going to keep putting in before you give up?"

If it's Twizzlers, maybe three, but if it's my father's

brain I'm going to empty my pockets. I'm gonna go home and iron my dollar bills and change everything I've got into quarters and once I'm broke I'll get a sledgehammer and . . .

"Well, I'm glad you understand, Terry."

Bozeki is already gathering the rest of my family into a small room off the main nurses' station. And this time she's not fooling around. Even from a distance I can see she's loaded up on ammunition to convince us of whatever it is this time. There are nursing supervisors, social workers, a chaplain, and Peter on the speakerphone.

"Are you there, Peter?"

Peter's there.

"Well, I must say this is one of the most clearly defined living wills I've ever seen," she begins.

Coulda fooled us.

The bottom line is, if they'd had the living will the night before the early morning beep, this meeting would have been to tell us he was gone.

"So does anyone have a problem with implementing it now?"

I say something about how our hope has turned to selfishness. We're keeping him alive for ourselves, but he's suffering.

"I can't imagine what it would be like if he's in there only able to hear us and not able to react at all," Danny says. "That's got to be torture."

He also notes that we are desperately grasping at the smallest signs of physical activity. "We're saying things like, 'He had a good strong cough today,' as if that is a good sign," Danny says.

When it comes to Will, I'm afraid the acceptance will take a dive but he rambles something about watching TV with Dad at the time of Nixon's death and how they talked about how he didn't have to prolong his death because he had a living will.

"Nixon had a living will?" someone says.

"Do we have to talk about Nixon?" I say.

"This is hard for me," Will continues. "But I don't want to see him go on like this. He wouldn't want this. He was a good person, you know. He always made sure everybody in the family was taken care of, everybody had food and a place to stay no matter what."

This is more than the doctors want to hear, but it's not more than we want to hear. We know all the ups and downs we've had over the years, we know all about the no-matter-what's, and how our father never forgot that these boyish men were his children. No matter what.

"Peter, are you still there?" the doctor says, using it as a tool to move things along.

"Yeah," Pete says. "I was listening to what Will was saying."

"He was a good dad," Will says, his voice trembling like that first day at the hospital when he showed me the slip of paper they had both used to scratch out a final thought.

We sit there quietly. Even the doctor, who's always in a rush, just lets her time sit there.

With the final decision hanging in the antiseptic air of a hospital, I try to picture what signing on the dotted line will lead to in an instance such as this. What kind of position have they put us in that we can end a loved one's life with the dot of an "i"? What is our responsibility now, to stare at him until he dies?

Then Bozeki says she wants us to think about making the move to hospice care—making the complete jump from cure to comfort. She wants us to sleep on it.

But I don't want to sleep on it. I've got enough problems sleeping as it is. "Maybe we can make a decision right now," I say.

We do.

"You'll like the furniture there," one of the social workers says. "It's very nice."

The chaplain mentions he's a war veteran like my father. Will tells him that my father recently talked about wanting to be buried in Arlington National Cemetery.

"Oh, shit," I accidentally say. This is news to me. Are we really gonna have to go to Virginia and the Tomb of the Unknown Soldier and the whole bit? That place is a field trip, not a resting place. It's a tourist attraction. They don't let just anybody in there, do they?

"No, they don't," Will says.

Back in my father's room, his eleven-year-old grandson, another Daniel Shine, is doing a jig to some old Irish music playing on the boom box. He's all knees and elbows and surrounded by tubes behind the IV stand. It makes some of us smile.

The chaplain pops in and corners me slightly. "Hope does not lead to selfishness," he says sternly. "Hope is never selfish."

Manufactured Fate

What's unspoken begins to haunt me.

By the time the meeting is over the sun has gone down and my wife and I stare out the black windows of the car for half the ride home. These medical get-togethers are always exhausting and this one particularly so.

We usually go home and stare at the television. I stopped watching the medical shows because it was like going back to a hospital with commercials, but even the cop shows have become unbearable—Sipowicz has got prostate cancer, when detectives on *Homicide: Life on the Street* aren't on the street they're investigating overzealous hospice workers. "I give up. Let's go to bed," is how the night usually ends.

Once in bed I try to concentrate on problems at work to relax me. That has to be a first. I write for a weekly news-paper so I think about deadlines and stories that I should be working on. My title is general feature writer so I have no beat to cover, no restrictions on who or what I write about. So my life is kind of a variety show. One week I may be researching the homeless and the next, Tony Bennett. At night I will try to dwell on a mistake or problem at work but my thoughts end up roaming back to the hospital: into the corridors, at my father's bedside, trapped in a meeting of doctors and nurses.

Christine works in a medical lab so she always comes to the meetings to guide us if necessary, but she knows my brothers and I have to make all the decisions. It isn't until we're driving back in the car like this that I start to second-guess everything.

"They take you right there and then they pull you back," I say.

"What do you mean?" she asks.

"When I kept questioning Bozeki about what the best possible scenario could be she started to waver toward the end, but I let it go."

"I heard it, too," Christine admits.

It has only been a matter of weeks, what if we gave him months, how far along could he come? I had asked Bozeki. She shrugged as usual, but as she talked offhandedly she said things like, he will always need help getting out of bed or sitting up in a chair. It just sort of slipped by everyone, but I was thinking, wait a second, all we've got going is vegetable talk and then suddenly—after we've all agreed to pull the plug—you lay out the picture of him sitting up in a chair on us. To us, that is an extraordinary vision. After weeks of the horizontal flop, to envision him erect, a plaid blanket laid across his skinny legs, a lost Brian Wilson smile across his face, my God, what we'd give for a minute of that.

I wanted to scream, "Would he be sitting up and looking me in the eye?" Is that really possible?

I stopped myself because my brothers were already sold on surrendering and Lord knows that is no small thing. If I started talking about him sitting up in a chair in front of Will, we'd still be back there, holding on like tourists in a dangling cable car.

"You see him," Christine says, bringing me back to reality.

Those are three simple words, but the night before, after we had stood silently gripping the railings on opposite sides of his bed for close to an hour, I used just as many to sum up the situation.

"He is suffering," I said, before walking out.

At first, words had been few at home too. My sentences short.

"How's he doing?" Christine would ask.

"Not good," I would say on Monday.

"No one's optimistic," I would say on Tuesday.

"It's almost over," I would say on Wednesday.

"Bad," I would reply on Thursday, leaving only one word hanging in the air, like that's all anyone needs to know. I acted like no one could understand what this is like except my brothers and me. By week two of this it felt like

I had two families—the old and the new—and I couldn't tie the pair together.

And if it was up to me I'd probably still be fumbling with the connections like a four-year-old trying to knot a pair of sneakers. But Christine worked with me, stretching my sentences until she became the confidant I needed outside the broken circle of my brothers and the hospital staff, where there is always a thriving tension.

I wanted to shelter my children from all of this but my daughter, Brynn, is a sixteen-year-old who does not want to be sheltered. "Let's go see Grandpa," she says. She had given him such a great big hug a few weeks ago when he stood in our living room, an embrace he could take home and sleep with and she will give him one tomorrow, squeeze him tight enough to get her love into his bones.

My twelve-year-old son, Dante, catches me when my loose ends begin to show. Talking on the phone to a car mechanic the other day I started explaining how the A/C was only blowing warm and I meant to get it in last week but my father is in the hospital and we don't know what's going to happen because the doctors keep telling us . . .

"Dad," Dante said, looking up from the kitchen table, "they don't need all that information."

Thank you.

My wife and kids have become like this life raft filled with the supplies I need to sort through not only the maze of medical decisions but also the frustrating thought that I have to pick a point when all my energy has to go back to them and my job.

At work, when I show up to try and pull my weight despite this mess, they know my input will be short-lived. The sympathy that pours out from the workplace in situations like this always wanes in a matter of days when everyone but you wants to get back to business as usual. Whether it's my own guilt festering or not, I can hear the snickering of "Everybody's parents get sick. He's got a job to do. When is he going to stop milking this?" Am I milking this like a big sacred cow, I wonder. Each day I step into the office I hear the murmur of the moo, the steady hum of enough is enough already.

Maybe that is why when the doctor finally says, "OK, this is it," we don't exactly jump for the release, but we don't quite man our weapons the way we did in the beginning, don't come out blasting with questions of who, why, what if?

Have they simply exhausted us?

I wasn't the only one who heard the reference to my father sitting up one day. Christine heard it, Peter heard it, Danny heard it, even Will heard it.

It's just that we are worn to the bottom of our souls and the words of him sitting up someday instantly go on the same pile with: "He'll be going home Friday," "Just wait till the swelling goes down," and "He's graduated."

The one that did it for me, that made me nod so quickly

for comfort over cure was when I asked Bozeki: "What about the aggressive rehab therapy that one doctor told us about?"

"The pulmonary doctor?" She frowned.

"Yeah, he was all pumped up. Telling us only a week ago that Dad was almost ready to be a candidate for aggressive therapy."

I had visions of him on treadmills and rowing machines and I felt like a fool when she notified me that he was only referring to therapy for the lungs, methods to strengthen his breathing beyond the meager inhales and exhales that he's currently managing on his own. That's what we were getting pumped up about? Breathing? That was the one feat he might, if he's lucky, one day master?

Breathing.

He has not been lucky and each of us can look to the moment his fate was sealed by some tidbit of information that managed to rise up out of this well-staffed chaos and slap us in the face one at a time. Maybe for Danny it was when we hired the nurse to do nothing but listen to the air, maybe for Pete it was actually seeing my father's steady signature on the living will, maybe for me it was the illusion that we all seemed to give up at the same time.

I think, as a family, we somehow made the right decision in choosing hospice by making nuisances of ourselves and asking so many questions that one or two turned out to be the right ones, but a part of me wants to run through the halls of the hospital, warning people that there seem to be tracks in the hospital similar to those in the workplace. They look at people on paper and say, "Oh, he'd be good in this position, let's move him up," or "He's stale. All of his superiors want a fresh face in his place. Let's move him out." Getting on the track to rehab or hospice is a thin line indeed. "I've seen a lot of these cases," the doctor says. Uh-huh, there goes another one.

Sitting up, or horizontal six feet under? Depends on what sales pitch the family gets. And the average person is not ready for any of this. We are not prepared for the etiquette, the ethics, the social behavior of a hospital. The only things we are prepared for are the gift shop and the snack bar.

So we struggle and muddle and do the best we can, but when I say that my father's fate is sealed, I am not relinquishing my part in all of this as if it is beyond my control.

I do mean, in the end, it is we, his sons, who seal his fate.

Weekend at Darnell's

Hospice beeps me first thing in the morning. "This is your hospice coordinator. I'm going to be overseeing the move of your father, Darnell."

My father, Darnell?

You know, you spend seventy-eight years on this earth trying to build a modest legacy as a good and decent man, serve your country and make a name for yourself, and then in a month's time the medical world turns you into a guy with a mustache named Darnell. How the hell does that happen?

Anyway, they're not moving him into the real hospice—the one with the nice furniture—because there are no beds available. So they're just going to move him into a room on a different floor in the hospital.

I ask if it's a different type of room, a special hospice room. "Not exactly," he says. "But it has a painting."

"That's something," I say. Exhaustion is leading to giddiness.

Will beeps me. I told him we're supposed to just be using the pager for the doctors, but he says he likes the way he can call me from anywhere, especially pay phones. "I love when a pay phone rings and it's for me," he says. "I could have you call me at Burger King."

He goes silent for a minute and then he remembers why he called. He's at the hospital and he suddenly sounds very upset. "I've been thinking about it, and they're just not doing enough," he says. "You need to talk to Dr. Kiki . . ."

"Bozeki," I say.

"You need to tell her nobody's trying anymore. They should be getting him up and walking around."

"Up and walking around?" I say. "Yesterday you were talking about him being buried at Arlington. Up and walking around? . . . It'll be *Weekend at Darnell's*."

"You don't understand," he says.

I understand what he's saying. Have we tried everything possible, are we giving up before he is? And those are questions that won't die with him. I know that.

And I know we are all going to think and say ridiculous things on the way to this end. It's inevitable.

By day's end, Will and I are back on an even plane. We leave the hospital together. There's a funeral home I had seen in the Yellow Pages that I had mentioned to him. "But it was just kind of a pencil drawing, so I better take a look at it," I say.

He says he knows where it is and I should follow him from the hospital. He's been driving Dad's Oldsmobile Cutlass Supreme and he wheels it like a ship as my father did—slow wide turns and full steam ahead.

As we tool up US 1, I remember what Danny had told me. "Now don't just pick out any one. Scout one out like they do movie locations. See if there is one with like an ice cream shop and a pizza place nearby."

"How 'bout a Tony Roma's Place for Ribs?" I say to myself as I follow Will into the parking lot.

I pull alongside of him, and we sit there like cops, cars facing opposite directions, windows down. Ben Folds Five's "One Angry Dwarf and 200 Solemn Faces" is playing on his radio.

"Is that Dad's station you've got on there?" I say.

"No." He laughs.

We've been living day and night with Dad's music, which has become our own now. Even patients in other rooms at the hospital are starting to shout out requests—

Nat "King" Cole, Sinatra, The Ink Spots. The music has been a saving grace.

The night Pete had talked about praying I recall afterward how I went into the living room at home, turned the lights off, and put on a Nick Cave CD that had touched a nerve with me recently. Sitting in the dark, drifting away, I wondered if the music has been my substitute for true spirituality and if that is a bad thing. All my life I have turned to it for guidance, reassurance, inspiration. It has not failed me and it is not failing me now.

"I've been getting back into music. I just bought a CD player," Will says. "It has one of those carousels that holds three CDs so I've been buying in threes—three Dylans, three Neil Youngs."

"Buying in threes. You are beautiful," I say.

As we've gone about our tasks at the hospital I've noticed that Will has left himself in the past a bit. He doesn't have his own ATM card or calling card and when we were putting stamps on envelopes one afternoon he kept licking them until I mentioned they were stick-on stamps and he casually seemed semi-shocked that such a thing existed. Whether it's only circumstance or he purposely has lagged behind the rest of us I am not sure.

The conversation turns toward the bunk beds we had in our bedroom as kids. Dan had his own room but the rest of us slept in two sets of bunk beds across the hall from my parents and it was Will's idea for us to never sleep in the same bunk more than a night or two in a row. "We'll just keep switching around, no order," he said. "None of us will ever have our own beds. That will be very cool."

So I was an eight-year-old boy without my own bed. And it was very cool.

"I haven't felt as cool since," I tell Will.

"Me either," he says.

And on Sunday nights when we weren't allowed to stay up late enough to watch *Bonanza* it was not uncommon for someone to drop from a top bunk to get a bump on his head (maybe that's why we're all a little off) so he could run to Mom, who subscribed to the theory that if you went to bed right after a knock on your head you may never wake up again. After a quick inspection of the bruise she would say, "Oh my, you better stay up for an hour. Go watch *Bonanza*."

"That wasn't my idea," Will says.

No, I'm not sure who gets credit for that. In fact, I think we discovered it by accident. You can't plan something like that, just as we could never have imagined we'd find ourselves reminiscing in a funeral home parking lot at dusk.

"What happened to all the elephants?" I ask.

Will squints, reaches over to turn the music down and says, "They're around."

The sun is dropping quickly and there are absolutely no other cars in the parking lot except an old blue station wagon. Perfect, I suppose, for making those midday pickups at the medical examiner's office.

"You going in?" Will says.

I look toward the building. It is blacked out except for the glow of a tiny doorbell. "It's a bit spooky. You wanna go in with me?"

He politely refuses. Mom is waiting for him to get back. "Told her I'd pick her up a Junior Whopper," he says, clicking on the ignition.

"I'm just going to sit here for a while," I say. "Maybe I'll come back at daybreak."

He drives off and then circles back around and shouts out a final word of advice.

"Daybreak," he says, without stopping.

Daybreak

I'm looking at my own imaginary watch as I enter the front door. "I've got like forty-five minutes to do this," I tell the funeral director.

"That's plenty," he says.

But for the first three minutes all I can do is look at him. The hair is his own, but it's all on one side of his head, his eyebrows look as if they're coming off a two-week bender, and when he talks, his tongue keeps shooting out.

I'm ducking.

He's talking pre-need discount. That's good. I know how these places can prey on people, so I want to keep it all business.

"If he dies today, we still get the discount, right?" I say. I'm stone-cold. No emotion here.

"He goes ten minutes after you sign you still get the pre-need deal," he says.

Beautiful.

Until he hits the details and I turn into a Boca Raton mom planning her only child's birthday party.

"These Mass cards are fine, but do you have any folders that match the sign-in book? Maybe something with an eagle and a flag since we're going with the patriotic theme."

We're in a small conference room, and when he walks to a tiny closet door, I assume it's to pull out some examples of matching napkins, but when he flicks the light switch, an enormous showroom illuminates in the background. It's like the feeling of awe I got walking into a car dealership when I was a kid. Reflections and sheen and virgin upholstery.

"As you see, we have various choices of caskets," he says. "Let's start over here."

But I've already started over here. The paint jobs are meticulous, like the new Mustangs. Brushed topaz, shaded Venetian bronze with a crepe interior. I run my hand across the hood.

"That's a sixteen gauge," he says.

I want to test-drive it. I want to pop the top, hop in, and squeal off to oblivion.

But the price is a little steep, so I keep moving down the

line. Numbers escalate as the craftsmanship and gauge increase. When the handles swing up, so does the price, and rounded corners are at a premium. I immediately think about how the smooth corners would cut down on wind resistance and be a big plus aerodynamically.

"Look at this," he says. "These are very popular."

He's pointing at the large praying hands sewn into the inside of the lid so when you open it up for the viewing it is the first thing people see from a distance.

"Nice touch," I say.

"And look at these engravings on the side," he says.

But who's going to really notice all this craftsmanship, especially when there is a dead person inside to look at?

I gravitate toward the midpriced models—$2,995 to $3,395—for several reasons. Number one: My father was a modest man. Number two: I remember that's about how much he spent on his Dodge Polara in 1976. And that had a vinyl top.

It's the veterans model so when the lid is up the first thing you see is the American flag. It's perfect and . . . "It's out of stock."

But as long as my father doesn't die today *or tomorrow* there should be no problem ordering one in time.

With that settled the lights are flicked out and we're back at the planning table. As long as everything works out with the army, we intend to have a military service and the burial at Arlington and also have a regular church service here in Florida. But at the moment, I can't seem to decide on where to have the local church service. There are two Catholic churches nearby. "Those are the main options," he says. "One is on the ocean."

"Right on the water?" I say.

"Right on the water," he affirms.

"Not across the street?"

"No, right on the ocean."

But then he mentions that the priest on the water is Italian and can be a little nasty. The priest at the other church is Irish and everybody loves him.

"Accent? Or does he just have an Irish name?" I ask.

"Accent," he says.

I'm thinking.

"You don't have to decide right now," he says.

"Yeah, because I might want to do a drive-by. That's how I decided on this place."

"You liked the way our home looked?" he says proudly.

"Yes, very much so." It's true, the pencil sketch didn't do it justice. Because in the Yellow Pages, everything is yellow.

He starts going through a rapid checklist. Motorcycle escorts? Open or closed casket? Newspaper obit? Airtray?

"Airtray?"

"For the flight to Arlington."

"Of course, an airtray, yes."

"One or two viewings?"

"Aaaa . . . two."

"OK."

"Is two good?"

"It's up to you."

"Two then."

Memorial booklet? Yes. Flower car? Yes. Acknowledgment cards? Yes.

Yes. Yes. Yes.

Organist?

No.

"You don't want an organist?"

No, I say, as if I'm adamant about it. As if I have an aversion to organists like some people have with mimes.

But I have no idea why I say no; I'm just going with my first instinct.

"OK," he says, but I can tell by his eyebrows he's not pleased with my decision.

"You said it was up to me," I say.

"That's fine," he says. "No organist."

Asleep at the Wheel

I've got to go to work. I tell the boss that "it's just a waiting game" now, so I might as well get back into working regularly.

But, as family spokesman, the first thing I do is start calling all my brothers to tell them I said no to the organist.

"Why wouldn't you want an organist?" Pete wonders. "You're losing it. As of today, you are no longer family spokesman."

Before I can call everyone else, hospice calls and wants to meet with as much of the family as possible as soon as possible. There's only me and Will now. No one else can make it on short notice.

Pete's back in New York, Danny's stuck in Port St. Lucie, Chris is tied up with his own business. Will and I have been trying to work it in shifts. If I'm not at the hospital, he is. If he's not, I am.

I call to tell him about the hospice meeting, and he tells me that he had a little fender bender the night before. "I fell asleep and hit the car in front of me on the way home from the hospital last night," he says.

Mom's been upset. He's been staying up late talking to her about Dad and then going to the hospital afterward. All along, we've been trying to spare her the details of living wills and pull-the-plug meetings, but at the same time Will has been gently informing her of the end we're all facing. "She asked me last night if she'd be allowed to be buried at Arlington, too," Will says. "I told her yes and she said OK. That's all she said, 'OK.' "

I say nothing and he continues talking. "The police gave me a ticket, but I think the car behind me bumped into me."

"But you were sleeping," I say.

"So?" he says.

"You gotta get some sleep," I tell him. "You're losing it." But what am I saying? There is no rest. We've got to get to the hospital.

"I got kicked out last night," Bill adds matter-of-factly.

"What?"

"They kicked me out of the hospital. It was after midnight and they said I had to go."

"But they can't do that," I say. "We're supposed to have twenty-four-hour access. We're hospice people now."

"I explained that to them but they didn't seem to understand. I didn't want to make a stink because, you know, people are trying to sleep. But I want you to call Dr. Kiki . . ."

"Dr. Bozeki," I correct him.

"Yeah, can you call her and find out what's going on?"

As far as Will is concerned I'm still the family spokesman so I give him my word, although I'm tired of talking to these people and allowing them the opportunity to make us feel like we're nuisances, as if it wasn't for us they'd be able to do their job properly. But it really irks me that they would run someone off who is doing nothing more than listening to the sound of his father's breathing in a dark room.

I know I won't be able to get Bozeki, but I have the card of a nursing supervisor who was overseeing the move so I call her and she is appalled. "No, you should be able to sit in there and eat McDonald's at three A.M. if you want to," she says. "That should never have happened."

She wants names, ranks, and exact times as if we're going to press charges or something but I tell her we just wanted to be sure about the rules.

While I'm on the phone with her I get a voice-mail message telling me the hospice meeting has been moved up two hours. I try to get Will but he's already left for the hospital. I assume he's going to visit my father first so I call the floor and ask the nurse who picks up if she could please give a message to my brother. "I don't know your brother," she says. "I can't be . . ."

I explain my situation, that we're supposed to meet with hospice but the time's been changed and I can't get ahold of him but he might show up there . . .

"That's not my job." She raises her voice.

"I know it's not but I'm asking a favor—"

"I'm not here to do favors," she says.

I start shaking and get off the phone with her but immediately call back. A different person picks up the phone so I ask to talk to the nurse who was just speaking to me because now I want to yell at somebody but she says there's nobody around and when she calls out from the station no one comes forward.

"OK, OK," I say. "Never mind."

That is the best thing to do, I guess. I know when you're going through something like this there's a good chance you might pick the wrong person to blow up at.

When I arrive at the hospital Will has been lingering,

but for how long is not important to him anymore. "The supervisor says you can eat McDonald's in here at three A.M. if you want to," I tell him.

"I don't like McDonald's," he says.

A hospice coordinator dressed in a long navy blue dress with gold buttons from top to bottom approaches us in the hallway and tells us she's just waiting for an office to become free so we can all sit down. "Will they have a speakerphone?" we ask, thinking of Peter.

She doesn't know but she goes to check at the nurses' station. The scratch of the nurse's voice immediately hits me and it's verified when she tells the hospice woman that she has no idea about what phones are where. "And why are you asking me anyway?" she barks.

The hospice woman walks away but I move in. "I don't have the strength," I say to her.

"What?" she says, already annoyed.

"When I asked you to do a favor for me and my brother earlier and you got nasty I didn't have the strength to get into it with you," I say.

She just glares at me, like what do I want from her? And I don't know. I, myself, am only just now finding my own sense of compassion for people in situations like ours. I can't put it into words for her but I guess all I want is that she not take her own disappointment in life out on me or my father or my brothers or the families and patients who pass through here.

"OK, it's free. I've got an office," the hospice lady says cheerfully.

It's a bit of a closet with a few chairs, and when she closes the door, Will and I start dropping sweat before she's even done digging out her papers from a leather satchel and lining them up on a small, cluttered desk.

"OK," she says, and starts asking us a million questions—two and a half hours worth. I feel like we're in "the box" on a cop show. She's asking about our life history— my grandmother's maiden name, where did they come from, how did your grandparents die? Are you Jewish?—I realize I know so little.

Another hospice social worker comes in, a tall gentleman whose knees take over the room when he sits down. He's all smiles and giggles and I wonder if we're now playing some kind of medical good cop–bad cop game.

"We're not holding out." I laugh. "We just don't know too much."

I'm a man without history. I don't know if it's because I never asked or if my parents never wanted to turn to the past or what, but I know almost nothing about my ancestors. I'm not even sure what nationality I am. Once my father told me I was part Irish and part German but I think he must have been drinking because normally he'd say, "You're 100 percent Irish, my boy." I believe after WWII he decided to axe the German bit and it only became heritage under the influence.

I have no memory of ever having grandparents. Both sets were long gone by the time I arrived. I think Danny met one of them, but I'm not too sure.

However, in my mind, there were a few facts of record passed on to the next generation. One was that my father's mother kept cans of chocolate syrup in the basement for special treats on Saturdays. The rest were about my mother's father, William O'Shaunessy. He owned a drugstore, maybe two, maybe a chain, you know how time exaggerates. Anyway, the way the folklore goes, he was a pharmacist and he had these stores but he was also like this roving mayor of Brooklyn. You know, high-stepping the streets, smoking big cigars, and leaving enormous tips with shoeshine boys.

And a lot of hat tipping, too. "Morning, William, lovely day."

Then the big buoyant reply from my granddaddy: "Yes, it's a lovely day, Mr. Scheffield, and don't you look exquisite this morn'. Here's a stogie to calm you while you wait for the train."

"Thank you, thank you, William."

I liked thinking about him roaming the town in that manner, being a calming and generous force in a Cheeveresque cocktail chattering society. But when it comes to whether he dropped of a stroke at the age of sixty-two or took a tragic fall at the beach cottage in the summer of '51, I haven't the foggiest.

"Do you know how to spell O'Shaunessy?" the woman asks.

No idea.

We are sweating profusely now, looking at the clock on the back wall through a valley that we've carved out between the towering knees of a hospice social worker, and the only question we jump up to answer is: Was your father a coal miner?

I have never been so sure about anything, except maybe not wanting an organist.

"No," I say. "Our father was not a coal miner."

Finally, the woman tells us they're ready to make the move to the real hospice facility. "Good, we heard the furniture is nice there," we say in unison.

"It is. You're going to love it," the tall guy says.

After several signatures, the hospice lady releases us and we take the first exit door we see for a quick escape. It leads directly to the stairs and we clomp down, anxiously anticipating the burst of light and fresh air at street level, but the stairwell cuts us off, won't let us go beyond the second floor.

We walk out into a wall of slate gray curtains and rows of IV towers. We are tangled in a maze and it gets so claustrophobic we're trying to lose each other. I look at Will and, on top of the sweat, his nose is running down his chin. "Jesus, try that way," I say, pushing off him.

"Hey, guys," a voice comes from behind us.

It's Andy and he's in all purple, just as we remember him. He knows better than to ask us how things are going but walks us into the open, taking me toward the center of that first day Bill summoned me to the hospital. *"It's me, your brother Bill."* It's been about thirty inchworming days now. There is the first room Dad was in, tucked in the corner, where I initially saw him beneath the TV, helpless but still robust. I see my hands clumsily trying to stretch his gown up around his neck, Bill popping up behind me.

We are drawn toward the room near the nursing station where they quickly moved him when the seizures were erupting. His grip was so powerful then, his eyes so crazy with fear.

"Will, Terry," a spry voice chirps.

It is Nancy, her round face smiling. She seems glad to see us, and our manner quickly changes from lost in a maze to "we just happened to be in the neighborhood and thought we'd stop in and say hi." Nancy is sitting at a small desk, its top completely covered with rubber tubes and gloves, except for the two tiny clearings where she props her elbows.

Her chin cupped in her hands, the grin vanishes to sincerity and she tells us how she misses our dad. "You knew him," Will says sincerely.

It is hard to remember someone who did. Since leaving this floor, he has had so many procedures, so much care, all from dozens of people who know only the symptoms and this odd bunch of sons desperately circling his bedside. Even those poking in his brain, even the doctor presently in charge of the case—pushing us through every decision— never knew him. "Did you hear how she referred to him?

'A World War II vet or whatever,' " Peter said after one meeting with Bozeki. "Why do we have someone like that? Where is his regular doctor?"

Yeah, he had one, but he pulled out of this mess long ago and we've got to go back, or downstairs or upstairs, to find any real connections. Andy and Nancy are here in the land of hope, where he was coming in for an operation, recuperating from the original procedure, sitting up and chewing steak afterward.

"I remember when he was up and calling your mom after the operation," Nancy says. "He was such a nice man."

"You knew him," Will says.

"I knew him," Nancy confirms.

History Lesson

My history is immediate. It is flush up against my face. It is these six people: Mom, Dad, Danny, Will, Chris, Pete.

The list ends so quickly it frightens me. My whole life is steeped in the action of these characters. In Danny, being almost a decade older than most of us, I watched trends transform with his persona. When he walked around with pointy boots and a pompadour I looked up and saw Elvis Presley; when he switched to sandals and shoulder-length hair I saw the sixties, even though I wasn't old enough to truly experience them. Bill took me to Vietnam. Chris, who was always tinkering in the garage, took me under the hood of a car. We were all in this together.

And then you walk away. I know now that it was only one more phase I was going through when I looked around our house one afternoon—I was twenty years old with nothing more in my future than part-time jobs and the local junior college—and heard the lyrics to a song in my head: "You're twenty-one and your mother still makes your bed and that's too long, that's too long . . ." Instantly, it was as if family dissolved for me. Everyone seemed like a stranger. They became the people I lived with but not the ones I grew up with. We were sharing a house and nothing else.

So I packed and made the move to Florida, got up and left like . . . "like you were going to walk the dog," my mother said in anger months later.

It was that easy then and it is that hard now. Being regrouped in this way, the hospital becoming this odd meeting center, the constant contact amid adversity with my brothers, it has been rejuvenating for some reason. The only thing missing is bunk beds. Over the years, I have closed my eyes and seen us all together and now I open my eyes and here we are. We are all together.

I like it.

How did we ever let this camaraderie slip away?

There is no hate among us, no love lost, no grudges. I know of no jealousies or devastating secrets. For the majority, there are not even miles between us, only this artificial distance we've created over time.

I know we replaced some of it by creating our own families, or at least trying to, but is that what happens?

Sure, we have changed. Peter is more commanding and optimistic than I recall, Danny hungrier, Chris quieter and less enthusiastic, Will more eccentric. None of us has set the world afire. Danny has his little job at Sears, I write for the paper, Will has taken himself off the road to care for my parents for the time being, and Peter sells expensive medical equipment but it's all inconsequential.

Though I left them all as a man, I remember them as children. That is when we *lived*. I recollect how one minute we'd be shooting pool and the next we'd be battling with billiard balls, tossing them at one another. I recall the abuse my body could take when a cue ball was hurled into the small of my back, and I dropped for but an instant to fetch back my wind, breathing deep and pulling in the thick musty odor of damp concrete in an unfinished basement. Pain never felt so good, nor so distinguishable from the pain I feel now.

But brotherhood does not end. I know that now. I know that it is stronger than the frequency of visits. It is rooted in us. It is not the past I yearn for; no childhood free-for-all fantasies. No, it is each of them individually that I miss. But I am certain that their parts have become the whole of me. They are in my voice, damn it, when I hear myself speak as you, Peter. And they're in my thoughts, Will, when I sit silently for hours thinking and thinking and understanding less and less. And in my frustration, Chris, when I go to lash out at someone for no reason, and in my heart, Danny, when I try so hard I can't give up even when I want to. I am each of you. We are one another, whether we like it or not.

During this ordeal Peter has been staying at our house periodically and the other day Dante said to me: "Dad, he's like you."

He sees it. Of all the people who come and go from this house, of all the people he watches on TV day in and day out he has never said that about anyone. He sees the connection.

It is all about connection, isn't it?

I visited my mother yesterday and sat with her as she ate a milky cream-covered Lean Cuisine off a TV tray. "It's my favorite," she said.

Unlike Dad, Mom's personality and demeanor have changed over the years due to her health problems and that is why I probably feel more distance from her. This ordeal seems to have zapped her of what little strength she had and her spirit seems so delicate now that I forget that she can still take me anywhere I want to go.

"What was that poem you used to always tell us? The one about the animal crackers or . . ." and before I can finish, her dry lips are parting and the words cover me like a pile of wet leaves: "I had dogs and pussy-cats and bears and lions, too," she whispers. "And elephants with curly trunks like any boy would do." And with each word I can feel the animals running wild in my stomach.

Oh, where else can she take me? Where else do I want to go?

Back to a fort made of sheets and card tables, back to racing office chairs in a factory the size of a football field.

Where do *you* want to go, Mom?

Back to a seaside hotel my father and she used to frequent when he first retired.

"I would always get up before your dad," she says. "I loved to read in the mornings but I didn't want to wake him so I would turn the bathroom light on and read by the light coming through the cracks in the door. Then when he awoke we would take a long walk on the beach. We liked that.

"We liked the same things."

It is a sentence she will say over and over in the coming weeks.

We liked the same things.

After my father first retired they traveled the country, and when they were home in Babylon they always had a table ready for them at the Yankee Clipper restaurant every Friday. When they finally decided to sell the house in New York and move to Florida they sold it to a young couple with one baby, a boy. "Just like us when we first moved into the house," my mother says. "Just me, your father, and Danny."

That was their beginning. Before Danny arrived my

father was a good enough golfer to seriously contemplate giving the pro circuit a shot but Mom says he forfeited his dream once she became pregnant.

My father always seemed so directed I never pictured him as someone who had sacrificed his dreams or aspirations for his family. It surprises and haunts me a little. Especially since the course I've taken in life has been sort of the opposite. When I first had children I had a good-paying, stable job managing a Walgreen's drugstore but felt completely empty. Without full consideration of what the consequences might be I quit to try and make it as a writer, a move that put us in debt. To this day, we would probably be better off financially if I stayed in retail, but it is only now that it is beginning to nag at me, that I'm beginning to wonder how selfish my own aspirations have been. Instead of sacrificing for my family I have made them sacrifice for me. My father always told me he loved me, but what did he think of me?

This afternoon Jill called the house. All of us kept missing her at the hospital. On the day she was to arrive at five-thirty she was delayed until later in the evening so she spent time with my father alone.

We were kind of relieved that we missed her because, although excited, we didn't really know what to expect. Will even exited stage left before her scheduled arrival. "What time is she coming, five-thirty? I better get moving." He laughed. But he wasn't kidding, and booked out the door.

We are odd that way, and other ways, too, of course.

But her voice on the phone is sisterly and warm. To ease my strain and try to fill me with some pride she says: "Terry, in every family there is always someone whom the brunt of the responsibility falls on because they are a little wiser, a little more patient but . . ."

But in this case it is me because I laid out the money for a beeper.

She also tells some good tales of an uncle Larry Shine coming to New York from Ireland after leaving the rest of his family impaled on fence posts back in the homeland, but I am more taken by her voice, her steady and reassuring tone even when I ask the time. "It's three-fifteen, Terry."

I want to get to know this voice better.

In my heart, I guess I know that the only thing that could prolong the closeness with my brothers is my father's suffering and that is not an option. It bothers me that this solidarity, pieced together by inevitable loss, soon will crumble quicker than a ten-minute oil change.

If nothing else, up to this point, as I watch each of us passionately struggle through the days, one amazing fact has revealed itself: We are good people.

I did not know that.

So why couldn't we build on this and make a little history up as we go along?

Other people do it.

In my head I keep trying to finish my father's sentence. *There is enough* . . . time. *There is enough* . . . love. *There is enough* . . . understanding . . . to get us through this.

Anyway, amid all this mishmash of sentimental crap, you know the one thing that's been driving me crazy since I've reconnected with my brothers? The one thing, above all else, that has been eating at me? The one thing that, whether you are talking about the past, the present, or the future, leaves me completely disconnected and alone in this world?

Of all my brothers, I am the only one going bald.

Minus Mayo

Today is a race.

Will is telling me everything he has to do and I'm telling him everything I have to do. We are dueling errands.

"I have to get to the bank," he says.

"I have to drop off a down-payment check at the funeral home," I say.

"I have to pick up Mom's prescriptions."

"I have to go to my own doctor's appointment."

"I have to get a haircut."

"I have to do a drive-by past the church."

"I have to get Mom's groceries."

"I have to check in on Dad at the hospice."

"I have to check in on Dad at the hospice."

"I have to get the oil changed in Dad's car."

"Oil change? Don't worry about that," I tell him.

"But he's got that warranty, and if you don't change it enough they can say, 'You didn't change your oil enough.'"

"Terry, maybe you better come with me anyway, because I've never been to one of those ten-minute oil change places and besides I want to give you a letter I wrote."

"A letter?"

"To the police department about that accident. I don't want to lose my Safe Driver's License so I need you to type the letter on your computer for me. Can you do that?"

Yeah, yeah, I say rolling back into everything else I have to do today—make an appearance at work, take Dante to his music lesson, call Arlington to verify the specifics . . .

And we're off.

By the time the day is done, it isn't done. It's about eight o'clock at night when I get a beep from Will. I stop at a pay phone in a strip shopping center in Boynton Beach.

"I never got the oil changed," he says.

"I'm glad you called anyway," I say, ignoring him, "because we've got to get a copy of Dad's will to a lawyer. The lawyer he had doesn't exist anymore. The phone's been disconnected. We really have to do this 'cause you know the horror stories, how they're always saying old ladies lose everything to hospital bills and you have to take certain precautions and . . ."

"Where are you?" he says, hearing the traffic in the background.

"I don't know, some shopping center," I say.

"You're still out running around." He laughs. "You've

got to get some rest. Let me tell you what to do. You get yourself two cheese Whoppers, a twelve-pack, find yourself a chair . . . and just sit there."

"Just sit there?" I start laughing until I'm crying and then I hear him . . .

We're both crying.

Then the connection is going bad. "Will," I shout, "can you still hear me?"

His voice gives a faint reply.

"Did you say one cheese Whopper or two? One or two?"

It is barely audible, but there is no mistake about it.

"Two."

Maybe we can comfort each other.

Good-bye, Dad

I am hungover.

The run will wake me up and allow me to sweat all that cheese, mayo, and charbroiled grease out of my system.

I think about leaving the beeper home during this jog through the neighborhood but I'm already clutching it in my hand like an unlucky rabbit's foot.

The day is bright, almost a white light, and I squint as a school bus holds me back from crossing the first main street off my block. A dog gives chase and I pick up the pace.

There is freedom in my steps today, and I think it is because I'm OK with it. There are a lot of days in a long life and on one of them you must die.

I keep going over my father's life in my head. So much good, so little bad. And the sheer length of it. He's lived through the twenties, the thirties, the forties, the fifties, the sixties, the seventies, the eighties, the nineties . . . Man, when you think about it that way.

Of course, there are the almosts that will haunt me. He's so close to a lot of milestones. I can hear myself in the future saying that he almost made it to eighty years of age, almost reached fifty years of marriage, almost . . . almost lived forever.

One more day for him is one more day for us. But these aren't days anymore. These are slabs of time that we stand in while he waits for God to come.

The drugs are doing the work now. He's in the comfort zone. And even if we are never quite sure of the doctors' intentions, I truly believe we are doing everything we can.

Avoiding the sprinklers on the corner of Ocean Avenue, I go wide. I'm running through the checklist in my head. Everyone has been able to tell him they love him and his eyes have miraculously returned the sentiment. The funeral home arrangements have been finalized. Arlington and all its glory are set to come. His cable bill has been paid.

Sure, the organist is still up for debate and that oil change has to be taken care of, but the main things are covered. I can hear a familiar song in my head. It is soothing and uplifting.

I weave for one more dog and wonder when this pager will vibrate, when will we actually confront it, and will the acceptance I feel now really hold up?

I don't want to wait. I am ready now.

"Good-bye, Dad," I say aloud as I try to sprint the last quarter mile. "You were a good dad."

After a cool shower my breakfast seems to settle in my stomach as it hasn't in weeks. On my way to work my eyes are focused on the road and the job to come.

The daily zombie look on my face that my coworkers have commented on seems to have vanished and after only a half hour at work, I'm already planning where I'm going to lunch. I wonder if pizza goes with this shirt I'm wearing.

Pizza goes with everything.

A tremor shoots up my leg. I fumble for the beeper and quickly press the button to reveal the number.

It's all too familiar. It's only Will. What the hell does he want now, I'm thinking as I dial the number.

"Hello?" I say. The voice is foreign to me. Do I have the wrong number?

It's the police. "Is this Terence Shine?"

"Yesss . . ."

"I'm sorry to tell you there's been an accident. Your brother Will is dead."

Part II

"It's not dark yet, but it's getting there."
—Bob Dylan

No.

I keep saying it but the policeman doesn't shut up. He's saying the things the textbook taught him to console me but his tone is so matter-of-fact it's even more disturbing.

He's talking over my shock. "How soon can you be here?" I'm sputtering—I'm spitting and spatting with mucus pouring from my nose and drool dropping from my mouth onto my hands.

"III'MM A'NNN HOU-R A-WAYY," I say, every word riding a tidal wave of emotion—coming out swelled and distorted—and everything being repeated three times. "I'm an hour away. I'm an hour away."

"Do you have a funeral home we can send the body . . ."

I'm spinning. Funeral home? Do I have a funeral home? I'm planning my father's funer . . . I can't . . . Don't tell me . . . No. No. No.

"What happened? What happened? What happened?"

The officer is trying to tell me but I'm stepping over his answers. "Fell in the bathroom . . . hit his head . . . loss of blood . . . your mother is alone here . . . Do you want to speak to her?"

Those stupid statistics are popping into my mind—more people are injured in the bathroom than any other room in the house.

But do they die? Do they die?!!

"Oh, Terry." My mother's voice is on the phone.

"Oh, Mom."

"Oh, God."

It's Bill

What am I going to say?

I'm fumbling through my wallet and coming up with a pile of confetti, scraps of paper acquired since all this crap began: dozens of doctors' numbers, funeral homes, social workers, hospice, insurance companies . . . I've got to find my brothers' phone numbers.

And when I do, I'm overwhelmed. Peter's home phone, cell phone, work phone, pager . . . Oh, where the hell would he be and what am I going to say anyway?

I stop myself, as if I just wait a minute it will not be true. I will never have to tell anybody this. I'm getting dizzy. I sit back. I sit up. I sit back. I sit up. As each minute passes I get closer and closer to the reality that I can't shake the truth. I've got to hold back my hysteria.

My fingers punch out Danny's work number. I don't know what I say but he reads the tone of my voice and stolidly asks, "Is he gone, Terry? Have we lost Dad?"

He, too, is prepared for my father's death. His voice is calm. He is ready. I can't hold on to it. "It's Bill. Bill is dead."

"Wha-at?!!"

I hear his wails of disbelief, a contrast to my muffled blathering. He is all shouts and anger. He has startled his coworkers.

"My brother is dead," he yells to quell their curiosity.

And the words shock me all over again. My brother is dead.

We are silent.

We are both an hour away and we don't want to budge. "Find a chair . . . and just sit there," I can hear Will saying as if it were only yesterday.

It *was* only yesterday. Was it only yesterday?

The policeman calls again, he is getting uneasy. I don't

know how long I was on the phone with Dan, how much time is dropping away. "I told you I'm an hour away. I'm on my way."

"You know your mother is here alone now," the officer says.

I know, I know. As he talks I am scribbling on a piece of paper as if I'm taking notes: mother alone . . . funeral home for Bill. It's as if I can't get this straight.

I dial Pete's home phone just in case he might be there. "Heey!" he says buoyantly. He has tried so hard to remain positive through my father's steady decline. I know he has struggled being so far away—trying to fly down on weekends with every time possibly being the last time he will see his father. *What if he dies on a Wednesday?* Each time we pick him up at the airport he rushes off the plane wearing his business suit, his hair moussed back the way only a New Yorker can still get away with. "Have you got a pair of sneakers I can borrow?" he always says as soon as we get out of the terminal.

I know his praying has been incessant. I know he's been trying to balance his obligations with a new job and he's stretched to the max. I know all this but I show him no mercy.

"It's Bill," I say, forgetting about his wish to be called Will. *He was always Bill.*

"Bill is dead."

As it continues to spill from my mouth I wonder where the soft phrases are—he's passed away, we've lost Bill—or why I cannot walk him through it—there's been an accident, it's really bad, there was nothing they could do . . . All the subtleties are somehow out of my reach. Bill is dead.

"What are you saying? He was going to pick me up at the airport this weekend. I just talked to him last night. I just talked to him last night. I just talked to him last night," Pete says, coming at me in threes.

"I know, I know, I know," I reply. "I did too."

This Day Is Over

And I can't stop talking to Will as I drive up the interstate. I am shouting over the radio, which is still tuned to some oldies station from the ride to work this morning when I was listening to Howard Stern. The harsh chorus from a Dylan song keeps rollicking: "How does it feel?"

Billy, Billy, why didn't you just give yourself a break? The late nights at the hospital, the falling asleep at the wheel. You told me you felt like just lying down for two days. Why didn't you?

How does it feel?

But I wouldn't let you, would I? And you wouldn't let you, would you? "As long as Dad is lying down, we can't," you said.

Oh, how does it feel?

It feels like shit. I want God on my side now. I want that

netherworld in all its glory. I desperately want some kind of belief. The music can't save me now.

Watching me shake, the boss had asked before I left work if I would let him drive me to the condominium. "I'm ready to just say this day is over and leave now," he said.

But I declined. "I'm OK. I'm pretty good with things like this," I said, lowering my head.

"But I don't want to be good," I said, raising my head.

And what the hell was I saying anyway . . . good with things like this . . . What could I possibly compare this to?

No one is driving now. I am just moving closer and closer.

Still Running

I am home. I am in my wife's arms, shivering. Our house is halfway between work and my parents' condo and stalling has become my M.O. We sit on the edge of the bed and I stare at the alarm clock on our nightstand. Even the digital numbers don't look right to me now. Sevens look like L's, fives looks like S's. The strange thought that the police will never find me here creeps into my mind. It's as if I'm a fugitive, on the run from my brother's death.

Can I hide here? Is it OK if I just disappear into my wife's arms?

I get jittery and start pacing along the edge of the bed,

making the cut at the end and moving up the other side until my path is as square as the zeros on that clock.

It is time. "You have to go to your mother," Christine says.

I realize that my constant stalling only puts a burden on those on the other end of tragedy. That cop is out there pacing, checking his watch, peeking out the curtains. My mother is shaking, replaying it over and over in her mind. God, what must it have been like for her?

"I have to go to my mother," I say.

We argue over whether I should drive, but I just force myself behind the wheel. I know everything is out of my control, but I continue to want to set the pace.

We get back on the interstate, and as I head up the entrance ramp trying to join the flow of traffic a Baskin-Robbins tractor-trailer impedes my progress. I am trapped alongside it, looking up at the semi-length mural of pastel ice creams and confetti and sprinkles that distract me for but an instant, and then I blank out until we are at the exit, heading east down PGA Boulevard.

The double doors of the fourth-floor condo are both wide open, propped by hat racks and a vase the paramedics slid over to accommodate the stretcher. I am so tired of having such easy access to doom. No one ever warned me that the gates of death would be flung open so freely.

The policeman is already in the kitchen "wrapping things up" with his superior on the phone. Will's body is long gone.

"He talked to one of his brothers on the phone around midnight," the officer is saying. "It looks like he must have gotten up in the middle of the night to go to the bathroom and slipped. The faucet was still running."

"I should have known something was wrong when I heard the water running," my mother's voice rises up behind me. Lost in myself, I keep forgetting my own mother. She is so fragile and as I take her in my arms there is nothing but a stiffness, a hard shell that feels like a body's natural attempt at armor. "But I thought he was shaving or something," she says, grabbing at her lips. "Oh, what happened? What is happening to us?"

I have no answer.

There's a sure wind shooting through the front door and out through the screens of the back patio toward the Intracoastal. The bridge is up and the tips of masts are steadily treading past. It is a relief that the air is not heavy.

The policeman hangs up and approaches me with the same stride as an officer about to give you a traffic ticket. I can tell he is more restless than uneasy. He's been babysitting my mom, his lunch has been on hold.

He's outta here.

"There's a bit of a mess in the bathroom," he warns us in parting.

I talk to my mom and try to get some sense of what happened. Her pacing back and forth . . . *Oh, he's just shaving . . . better leave him alone* . . . the anxiety building . . . *Oh, what could be taking him so long . . .*

"I should have known something was wrong," she says, pulling at my arm. "Is the water still running? Is the water still running?"

She has blocked out the details but says something about trying to wake him and repeating his name over and over. Not his new name, but the one she would call from the back steps of our yard in Babylon: "Billy, Billy, Billy!"

I can only envision her dialing 911, poking her fingers at the numbers and mumbling into the phone for help. And then what did she do? Did she crawl up beside him? Did she want to run? What kind of eternity is the six-minute response time when your son is lying on the bathroom floor between life and death?

"If Daddy was here this never would have happened," Mom says. I want to block the thought out but I can't help thinking she is right. Dad wouldn't have allowed this kind of shit to happen. Not on his watch.

She keeps saying she should have done something but from what I can sense and what the police said, knowing "something was wrong" when she awoke in the morning wouldn't have saved him. The night took him away.

Danny arrives and we embrace; there is little to say. Little Daniel is with him, and I curse under my breath that he has to come to this place, but Danny had to stop and get him out of school because he didn't know when he'd be home again. Between this and the dreary hospital visits, what must this boy be thinking? I want to command him to stare off at the yachts and catamarans and the high-top sport-fishing vessels with their flimsy rods pointing high into the clouds. Stare at the ships until everything is right in this world again and I tell you to turn around, and not a second before.

Christine goes to the kitchen closet and we all mechanically go about setting up to clean the bathroom as if it is our only chore left in life, as if we can wash this all away.

We are operating so meticulously. Making sure we have everything before opening the bathroom door—mops, brushes, bleach—because there can be no turning back.

We move in a flurry, our brains as empty as those of noontime maids at a thousand hotels. We can't think about why we're doing it. The blood is dark and forbidding but it's just a job. Just do the job . . .

But then I pour the bleach liberally and we're overtaken by the fumes. I grab on to the bathroom counter to steady myself, Danny grabs on to me and we both end up stumbling out the doorway and collapsing on the floor.

"We need to let that clear out," Christine insists. But then I get up, head back in, scrub what I can, and then dash out the door. Danny sucks up a deep breath and goes in as I come out rushing to the balcony for air. We're working like a frantic tag team.

It's as if we're trying to put out a fire, as if there are lives to be saved. But there is nothing to save here. We just want to wipe it out.

We should wait. We should let things soak, let the solvents go to work, but we can't. I'm gagging and my eyes are gone but I'm scrubbing, scrubbing, scrubbing.

Then it turns into a fight. The blood clots won't go down the drain in the bathtub. They're swirling and swimming away and I'm jabbing at them with the broom, trying to break them down, trying to herd them toward oblivion. Danny is slipping and leaning in. "Let me do it, let me do it," he says, grabbing at the handle.

Our four hands grip the skinny wood and shove and shove until we are groggily standing side by side watching the last of our brother's blood disappear.

Stop It

I am lying in bed staring at the ceiling as if it is the sky, as if it is that great expanse you can look into to try and find some reason, some consolation. But it is straightedged and confining, closing in on me.

Pete has just called again to let me know his plane hasn't left Philadelphia yet, something about torrential rains. I envision a tumultuous raging storm covering all of us. Right after I called him earlier today he searched for the first flight out of New York that he could find but it has turned into a long night's journey. All of his family is in Florida. He's single, traveling by himself, and I don't think he's close enough to anyone in New York right now whom he could call on for comfort. I pity him alone with his thoughts.

How could he stand under the industrial lights in an airport terminal listening to the idle chatter, the revelry of first-day vacationers, the no-nonsense tones of businessmen on their cell phones. And what face does he wear when someone approaches him with monotonous small talk and how does he avoid spilling it out to some stranger with a compassionate face?

We don't talk about what he is thinking or why he is coming or make any small talk of our own, we only discuss the logistics of getting here. "I'll call you when I land in West Palm," he says.

We took little Daniel home with us because Dan is presently sleeping within a few feet of our mother. I didn't want to stay there, listening to her tell us how Will would always keep the door to his bedroom open at night so in case she fell he would hear it. I am strangely afraid of her memories of what has transpired. I liked it better when she initially blocked out the details. I am not as ready to hear them as she is to say them, if that makes sense.

Rain begins plunking on the aluminum awnings outside my own window and I follow its sound until it turns from soft to hard and then I roll over to face the wall.

It is all written there, nothing is left to the imagination. Nothing in this day can be erased, I know that.

The fatigue takes me to sleep, but my own absence is short-lived. The phone is ringing. It's 2:30 A.M.

It's Peter. "I'm here," he says. "Do you want me to just take a cab to Mom's?" I want to be with him but I can't move.

"Yes," I say.

I keep trying to block it out but one thought keeps popping into my head. It was only a week or two ago, during the whole living will fiasco, when Will mentioned to me that he, too, had a living will. "Next time you're here I want to show you what drawer it's in," he said. "Don't be silly, you're not going anywhere," I said. "I know, I know, but just in case, you should know where it is. I want to show you exactly what drawer." Irritated, I kept cutting him short. "Stop it," I demanded. "Stop it. You're not going anywhere."

I'm trying to put these thoughts on hold. I am strangely afraid of my *own* memories.

Sleep comes to save me, but the respite is cut short once again. The phone is ringing. It's 4 A.M.

"Terence Shine?" the voice says. It is a gentle voice that slowly separates me from sleep, and I immediately grasp that my father has just died "quietly and comfortably," not with a "slip and a thud," yet I know instantly there will never be any separating one death from the other. The day itself will forever be a ghost.

But I immediately find solace in the fact that neither of

them had to hear that the other died. "Isn't that some-thing?" I turn to my wife. No one in this world ever got the chance to say to my father, "Mr. Shine, your son is dead." No one got to say to my brother, "Will, your father is dead." They never had to hear the words that surely would have crushed them.

But now I have to call Peter and Danny and tell them that they have lost both their brother and their father within twenty-four hours. It is not the kind of ending to my family spokesman act that anyone could ever have anticipated and the thoughts in my head keep making me hesitate.

The last thing the hospice woman quietly asked me on the phone was if anyone wanted to come see the body before it was released to the funeral home. I had no answer for her but she stuck that word "body" in my head.

That's all they are now. Two lifeless bodies lying out there in the night. Their individual characters zapped and reduced to nothing more than bodies that need to be tended to, bodies that need to be dealt with.

Danny picks up the phone, his own voice worn into a solemn softness. He assumes I'm calling to see if Peter made it OK. I can hear Peter rustling in the background, fumbling with one of the pullout couches. "Ahh, I'll just leave it shut."

Naturally we had blocked out thoughts of my father as we went through the motions of this day and only secretly hoped that he would not pick the one time we were unable to be at his side as the day to leave us.

Danny starts talking pillows and blankets as they continue to set up camp and I latch on to this diversion and use the conversation to sum up his situation. Is Peter nearby to reach out to; is my mother sleeping?

"Danny, the hospice just called."

And the words do not come from my lips. I leave him to tell himself, to grasp at a chair to steady his legs, to pull Peter close, to whisper to his mother. To lay his body down on an old couch for the few remaining hours left till dawn and stare at the ceiling as if it is the sky.

It's Bad

I must have turned the lamp in our bedroom on in the middle of the night and never shut it off because as dawn starts coming through the windows the natural sunlight only seems to pile on to the artificial, drowning it out.

Hospice calls again since I haven't responded to the question of whether anyone wants to come see my father before he is turned over to the funeral home. I rack my brain. Was there a certain protocol involved, was there something I missed in the pamphlet or while I was a sweaty mess trying to map out our family history? Did the counselor say: "Now be sure to see the body before it's taken away. That's very important." Or is it only one more precautionary measure? One more box they check off on a form: __ Family given opportunity to see deceased before being removed from facility.

I want to do the right thing. If I gave Peter the option would he jump on it, would he crawl into the car early this morning and stroll the quiet of the hospice's pleasantly decorated hallways toward the stillness of his father? Or would I just be burdening him, adding one more piece of pressure to crack him open? To be there in the end is one thing, to see the end is another.

I tell them no. I will not give any of my brothers the opportunity to pain themselves any further.

Chris, who doesn't have a phone, doesn't even know what's occurred. It is my first stop today, and as I drive our blue conversion van toward his small white-brick apartment near Federal Highway the tires hit gravel and it's one detour after another. Flashing lights and a blockade stand at every corner leading to his street. I am finally being boxed in the way I always wanted, finding it impossible to reach my destination. But it's too late, isn't it?

Fed up, I squeeze around one of the barricades, churning up the white powder of a fresh construction site, and creep toward the string of four apartments.

I don't know which one he is in. My own brother and I've never knocked on his door, never dropped him a note in the mail. Damn it! I start banging on one door and running to the next and *bam! bam! bam!* as if I'm trying to alert sleeping tenants to a fire. "Chris, Chris, where are you?"

I see the mailboxes off to the side, every one has a name on it except number one. He's in number one; he's in number one.

I bang on number one again and Chris opens the door, allowing just enough clearance for my body to slip in. It is a warm and suddenly cloudy day and the place is as stuffy as a closet full of winter coats; his windows are sealed and the lights are off. He makes no effort to turn them on, so we stand in the middle of the room with nothing but the crack of gray light coming through the door. As my eyes adjust I look up at his thin profile, a frightened but prepared look in his eyes. "Something bad has happened," I say.

"Something bad?"

"It's bad."

I guess I'm trying to make up for the way I jolted my other brothers with the news but it's as if the words are stuck; not in my throat, but deep down in some place I've never been, some place I'm so unfamiliar with I don't know exactly how to retrieve them. I thought notifying people would get easier but easy is nowhere to be found.

"It's *bad*, Terry? *Terry*, it's bad?"

"It's bad. It's real bad."

The mundane banter is choking me. Everything is going black again, as if my eyes have only this second entered the room. Lost in the dark, I reach out, swiping my arms back and forth to be sure Chris is still there in front of me.

"Bill is dead," I say.

I keep my eyes adhesed to his shape, as if he might disappear into the darkness. He is silent and as time passes I assume we are in that moment of absorption, that moment of reckoning, and I count seconds off in my head as if he is allowed a certain amount of time to take in one death before he is handed another.

"And Dad, Dad is gone," I say.

I don't even realize until later that he asks for no explanation about either. He has no need for circumstances.

"I'll be out in a minute," he says, walking toward his bedroom.

We drive back into the cloud of dust that still hasn't settled from my arrival and after about fifteen or twenty miles on the interstate Chris says, "I think I better go home. Could you take me home, please?"

I look in the mirror and it is as if he is sitting in the back of a taxicab. Chris has seemed oddly detached since this whole ordeal with my father being in the hospital began and I don't know whether he is just in shock or has problems I know nothing about. I hold my breath for an instant and Christine reaches out to hold my hand and grimaces. We don't know what to say.

I ignore him and keep driving, turn the radio up to a song to which the only lyrics seem to be "Thank you." *Thank you, thank you, thank you,* a sweet voice sings.

Christine and I choose the outdoor stairway and start trudging up the four flights to the condominium. Chris lags behind and as I reach each floor I look down and see his hand gripping the railing of one landing beneath us.

Peter is in the shower. There are two bathrooms and I can't believe he chose the one we were scrubbing yesterday. I hear the blast of the pulsating water massager echoing off the fiberglass tub and I am dumbfounded. To the naked eye I know we finally cleaned it up as good as new by day's end but in my mind it is still as filthy and stained as can be.

"Hey!" he says as the bathroom door opens and he scoots into Will's room, holding a towel around his waist with one hand, a blow-dryer with the other, the brown cord skipping along the carpet as if it's trying to keep up with him.

Danny has a strange grin on his face and Christine and I give each other a baffled shrug. "Very cavalier," Christine says softly.

"He's something, isn't he?" Danny says. "A brazen son of a bitch."

He's something all right. Maybe since he wasn't part of the clean-up crew . . . I don't know . . . maybe he's blocking it all out . . . whatever . . . but if we're ever going to make it through this we probably need at least one brazen son of a bitch among us.

I go back to the front of the condo and swing the double doors open again. "What are you doing?" Christine asks.

For some reason I thought that's how it would always be in this place now. To keep it from becoming stifling, to keep yesterday from smothering us, we would never close the doors again.

Danny walks over and closes the doors.

The second the zoom of the blow-dryer stops Peter is in the living room and I start blabbing about how now we've got two bodies out there and . . .

And my mother is standing stiffly in the doorway of her bedroom, her face a mask of devastation. The stoic reserve has completely left her and she has been stripped of the natural armor her body allowed her yesterday. I am crippled by the sight of her and when I avert my eyes to my brothers they look at me as if I have just broached some kind of taboo by mentioning the deaths.

"Mom didn't know about Dad," Danny whispers.

She was finally sleeping after taking a sedative last night and Peter and Danny didn't want to wake her to tell her about my father's passing. Now she knows. The word riding in on my insensitive blabbering.

We are crowded in her living room but her world, her everyday, has been blown away. The two people she woke up to each morning, the two people who cared for her on a daily basis have now been replaced by this "What to do?" committee of sometimes children. I go to her but she brushes me away. "I just want to lie down," she says.

I cannot chase her back to her bedroom and embrace

this away. I have no idea what to say or do. "I love you," I mutter.

The phone rings and it's a social worker who heard about our situation. He wants to know if he should send over a grief counselor. I look out at my family, their feet pacing on the faded brown carpeting, and I can't imagine them settled in a circle concentrating on sorrow. "I will have to get back to you," I say.

I open it up to discussion but nobody seems to want to even deal with the question, let alone the intrusion. I am the only one who wants it, but my reason is because I think others might need it, especially my mother.

"What are they going to tell us, huh?" Peter demands.

We all go silent and I think of what a shame it is that America's gluttony for support groups has turned them into a cliché-ridden sham. We can immediately envision the rehearsed sentiment: *"You must be devastated. How many of you are angry? Are you angry, Terry? Well, let me tell you something, it's OK to be angry. You've all heard that time is the greatest healer and it truly is and* . . . And the clipboard resting on the counselor's knees will rise up and there will be one more checklist to go through. *"Now, how many members of the family are there? Are they all present? And you're the oldest, Danny?"*

And it's a shame that perhaps when someone could really use the help, we can't get past the fact that the idea of support has become a joke.

So we might as well excuse ourselves and turn to the responsibilities that are facing us. We've got two bodies to deal with and we don't know how we're even going to pay for all of this.

"How many plane tickets to Arlington are we going to need?" I say, starting a head count. "And then if we have to stay overnight and food and . . . We're talking thousands of dollars to pull it off."

My mother returns to the living room and sits in a captain's chair at a small round table. "Whenever anyone else died, I always had Daddy," she says. "When my mother and father died, Daddy was there for me, when my sister died, Daddy was there for me, when . . ." She shrivels up into the chair, pulling at the sleeves of her sweater and her mind seems to drift away but then she looks at me and says, "My brother Terry. That's what Billy would say to me when he came back from the hospital. He'd say I went to see Dad and my brother Terry was there. He always said, 'My brother Terry.' "

She laughs softly when she tells us he didn't recognize me the first time at the hospital. The experience was mutual, I guess. How strange did I look to him? My hair disappearing, my chin obviously doubling despite the goatee's meager attempt at camouflage.

Peter mentions that he thought Chris was a social worker or something when he first encountered him in Dad's hospital room. "I was waiting for someone to introduce us," he says.

"I thought you and Dan were orderlies," Chris says to me.

"Orderlies?" we chorus.

"Well, I'm going to go call work to tell them I'm never coming back," I say, changing the subject.

"I'm next," Peter says.

I walk into Will's room where a plain white phone sits atop a plastic TV tray near his bedside. There is a pad of notes next to it and it is filled with questions and incidents we had talked about during the past week. I guess he kept a list of reminders so he wouldn't forget what he wanted to ask, just as I tried to do, so unsuccessfully, with the physicians. Scribbled in black ink are things like: Tell Terry about being asked to leave hospital, is that right? Why isn't a physical therapist working with Dad? Pick Peter up at airport if no one else can. Ask Peter more about Coumadin . . .

On and on until I reach the last thing on the list, something that must have been eating at him since he bugged out of the hospital that one afternoon. There, with each word underlined, is the question: Did anybody catch wind of what Jill was driving?

While I'm on the phone to work I recall how Will insisted he had to show me that drawer with all his important papers. I turn around and smile at the fact that this is a room with only four drawers. Life was simple here: a TV, the new CD player, an antiseptic white recliner aimed at the boat masts to the south, and a waist-high bureau with four small drawers, each lined with plastic and filled with T-shirts and briefs folded military style.

Mixed in with the tightly rolled socks, my hand falls on what from this point on will be known as "the brick"—a neatly packed bank envelope with $10,000 in $100 bills—some with big Ben Franklin heads, some with small.

I have so many doubts about every move we make during this time of mourning but this is one thing I am sure of: Money is for the living.

"Whoppers for everybody," I mutter to myself and then to the crowd in the living room.

At first it is a joke, but then orders are being taken and a team is heading out with a crisp hundred-dollar bill.

"Minus mayo," I shout after them. "Will always minused the mayo."

When the overstuffed bags arrive we begin reverentially passing the Whoppers around like the final offering of a loved one. I want to eat two, but I don't know if it is possible.

Mouths are straining to open. For some of Will's nephews it is their first experience with the mammoth burger. "The Whopper is a rite of passage," I tell them. "No more of that Happy Meal crap. You are men now."

The room is filled with the sounds of crunching down on charbroiled patties topped with mounds of moist lettuce, slippery ketchup, overripe tomatoes, and onions. The only sound missing . . . is the mayo.

How Many Pallbearers?

The funeral home wants an appointment for two o'clock.

"We've got to talk," they say.

No kidding.

Chris volunteers to stay with Mom and the rest of us pile into the van to make the half-mile pilgrimage.

Jesus, I remember me and Will parked like lazy cops in the funeral-home parking lot; listening to Ben Folds Five, staring at the glowing doorbell and talkin' shit until the sun went down. He was afraid to even walk in the front door and now those bastards have got him in there on a slab.

When I see the place again I start shaking my head in disbelief, which I guess I will be doing forever. The white columns and simple black trim, which I saw as classy touches on the building a few days ago, now reek of horror, the blackened edges a symbol of how our world will be tinged with darkness from this point on.

The morticians have "Woo-ee Tandem Funeral!" written all over their pale faces. They royally lead us into the main conference room as if we're out-of-town high rollers. If this were Vegas we'd get a comped suite for throwing our business their way but in this case it's only no waiting and refreshments we politely refuse.

Right away my brothers start tearing into my previous plans. "These folders are all wrong," Peter says.

The funeral director makes a face as if he knew they were a poor choice all along. "Why didn't you give me that face?" I say. "Maybe I would have gone with something else. You should have given me that face."

"I was trying to be kind." He smiles.

"We better see those caskets again," someone says.

"You don't think your father would have wanted an organist?" the director asks the group, like some kind of school-yard tattletale.

"Hey, I already told everybody about that," I say.

"We want an organist," everyone choruses.

For some reason we are acting stupidly giddy. It's as if it's a relief to be in a funeral home, which makes sense, I guess, since our lives are currently about nothing but death. Why shouldn't we feel most comfortable in a funeral home? Here we don't have to worry about how we're dressed. We can dispense with the small talk, make up our own rules and regulations and not have to worry one bit about merging into someone else's lane. All will be forgiven and accepted in the name of grief. These are our people. We have nothing in common with the living anymore.

"Where are the cards, those laminated things?" Peter says. "Those . . ."

"The Mass cards, of course, let me show you the choices," the director says. "Your brother didn't think they were necess—"

I cut him off with a stare as he scatters some examples

across the table and everybody reaches out as if we're playing Go Fish. There are Joseph and Mary cards and sheep cards and one that is nothing but clouds; another has snowcapped mountains reflected in a blue-black lake.

I am lost in the clouds when he says, "Perhaps an assortment," and everyone agrees.

After the finishing touches on my father's arrangements the sale turns to Will and I am prepared to shut it down quickly.

Earlier in the day, after I had discovered the brick, I also found Will's private papers—the ones in the drawer he was going to show me—and they turned out to be nothing more than a couple of handwritten notes but they were very clear. "Don't keep me alive on machines and cremate me as soon as possible."

"Oh, no," Peter says. He's very much into putting people on display. "Why would he want that?"

"That's what I want when I die," I say, and he looks at me like, fat chance of that if I'm still around, buddy boy.

I've always felt cremation was a dignified, affordable alternative, I argue. No embalming, no casket, no hoopla, no fanfare, NO FUNERAL HOME. "All people would have to remember you by is your life," I say.

"Wouldn't that be awful," Peter says.

The funeral guy reminds us that we can do both. Have him at the viewing and then cremated afterward. The ol' rent-a-casket thing.

As far as I'm concerned Will wouldn't have wanted to

be showcased at all and Danny agrees. "We shouldn't do that to him," he says.

"But he never would have known he'd have the opportunity to be put on display with Dad, not in his wildest dreams," Peter argues. "He wouldn't want to pass this up."

That's true.

I waffle on the quick cremation in the same way I folded up—and stuck in my back pocket—my initial belief to immediately show my father's DNR order to the doctors after I actually read it. There seems to be no place for long-held convictions in the face of death. Up close, my previous views on what's right and wrong need not apply.

And anyway, how would it feel to hold a viewing and funeral service without Will there? There is a mysterious bond tying this father and son together for all eternity, so who am I to try and break it now?

But to walk into a room with frilly curtains and cherry-wood pews and see the two of them lying in boxes "lids up" would be unbearable for me, I confess.

I may be selfish but I could not handle that, I keep saying.

"OK, one open, one closed," the funeral director says, putting his hands together in a soft clap.

And Peter can lift it open and peek whenever he wants as long as he notifies me first.

The director gets an example of a plain wooden urn and we pass it around the conference table like that gold phone in *The Godfather Part II*. Some are surprised by the weight, a couple linger with it in their hands, others pass it on quickly.

"Oh, the mustache," Danny remembers. "We need to have you remove my father's mustache."

Not that it doesn't look good on him.

No problem, as a matter of fact the mortician would like photos of both the deceased to use for reference.

"OK, how do you spell your mother's maiden name?" the director asks.

Aaaa, we'll have to get back to you on that one.

Obits are the next order of business and my father's goes smoothly with lists of his war medals and corporate job and retiring to Florida, blah, blah, blah . . .

But with Bill we're a bit hesitant. No one's quite sure about that service record. "Oh, he was in the service, too?" the director says. "During the viewing we can drape a flag over his casket, too. Do you have a copy of his discharge papers?"

No, we don't have his discharge papers, and besides, maybe Will wouldn't want to be draped in the American flag. "OK, what did he do for a living?" the director continues.

Well, that's kind of iffy, too. Lately he'd just been hanging out, buying CDs in threes, and collecting hundred-dollar bills.

"Was he civic-oriented?" the director says before we can finish a thought.

"He was big in the Jaycees," I say, getting a cheap laugh out of my brothers.

But the director starts to write it down, and it dawns on

me that people just make up obits. That's why the notices always say he was a former Navy SEAL. Families must blurt it out under pressure to make their loved one's lives seem interesting. It's one more example of how none of us ever accomplish enough in the eyes of the people close to us. Even a good life demands embellishment. And besides, nobody checks these things. As long as you give the newspaper its $137 for 42 lines of copy it could care less. That's why three out of every four obits start off with how the deceased attended Juilliard and West Point before going into the watch business for forty years.

Peter seems to catch on, because before you know it he's bragging about Will's trucking business. Sure, he drove a truck for a while but there was no business or any . . .

"What was the name of the business?" the director says with his pen racing across a page of yellow legal paper.

"Will Shine Trucking," Peter says proudly. And I can almost see the fleet of Macks with custom sleepers heading up the turnpike in a caravan.

Peter also takes the time to explain to the director that our brother went by Will. "Will is what everybody called him," he says, like it's been that way since he was born, not just for the past three weeks.

"You mean like 'Will,'" the director says, his fingers clawing quote marks into the air.

"Yes, yes," Peter says. "This guy's got it."

The director scurries off to type up the obits, and when

he returns he places them in the center of the table for our approval.

William J. Shine

"Will"

We love the quote marks and the capitalizing. It looks like a little WILL billboard. And when we get to the line that "he had been a resident of the Palm Beaches since 1990 coming from Babylon, L.I., New York, where he owned and operated Willshine Trucking . . ." we are ecstatic.

It would have been a great company.

"And the way they made it one name—Willshine. That's a nice touch," Peter whispers.

Proofreading my father's obit we see that he's listed as Daniel L. Shine Jr. "He never went by junior," I object.

"His father was senior, he's junior," the director says as if it's all so cut-and-dried.

But as far as I know senior was a bit of an absentee father. I remember how I always thought he had died young like my father's mother because there was never much talk about him, but apparently he had a full life, just not as a parent. There are probably hundreds of stories about how he drank up his paychecks and arm wrestled coworkers atop crates at the loading docks near Battery Park but I was never privy to a single one about a father and a son. That is why I am always amazed at what a natural my own father was at being a dad, a role he excelled at with no solid points of reference, a job he learned from no one.

I guess what I'm saying is: "He was nobody's junior."

"Fine," the director says, making a little x over the Jr.

With that settled there are only the matters of thousands of dollars and pallbearers.

Pallbearers?

"You'll need about twelve," he says.

Oh, shit.

"We don't have much family down here," I say.

"Oh, you have friends," he says, ushering us toward the door.

"No, I don't."

He chuckles, but I am serious. Even Dad used to always say, "You may have a lot of acquaintances but you don't have many friends." I'm counting on my fingers a couple of possibilities but I'm not really up to recruiting.

I have always prided myself on keeping my world fairly small but if I'd ever known I was going to need twelve pallbearers in a pinch, I would go back and change everything: I would pick up the check at every lunch I've ever eaten, I'd tell engaging stories to unengaging people, I'd talk to strangers in check-out lines, I'd wave back to my neighbors, I'd grin like an asshole when people slowed in front of my house while I was washing my car and said, "Hey, you can do mine next," I'd ha-ha right along with everyone in this fine nation if that's what it would take.

But it's too late now.

We're doing the math. Does he mean twelve for each? Do both have to be carried into the church at the same time or can we bring one in and then go back and get the other the way you do when you get your groceries from the car?

"You can always pay the Knights of Columbus," the director says. "But you don't want that."

We don't want that.

"This is wrong," Danny blurts out.

At first I think he is referring to the pallbearer thing or one of the other decisions we had to make. "No. Bill. This isn't right. He should be here."

We are not the type of people to say "Why us?" Why should we be in this freaky position? All he is saying is: This is wrong.

And I watch as he turns away from us. There will be no more jokes or kidding from him. I know our antics have been mounting; the odd playfulness that carried us through the weeks at the hospital has worn thin. It has reached its end with Danny. He's seeing the Whoppers and the shuffling Mass cards and the phony obits as the pitiful distractions that they are. His face is going in the other direction and the expression it settles into is startling to me. No matter how many times you see happiness or sadness or pain in a person's face, there is nothing to prepare you for the look of swollen grief that takes the place of every wrinkle and feature. It is spreading through the room and with all my trepidation about seeing the look of death on Will and Dad, I now realize that it could never compare to the fright

I feel seeing the faces of the living in the wake of the death of someone they deeply love.

"This is wrong," Danny says.

My Sign?

We're in the stairwell outside my mother's condominium—out of sight, out of earshot. We're not sure what she can handle. She seemed stronger than the rest of us after the first day or so, but I think it was because she somehow detached herself from the situation. We'd be talking about what happened and she'd be asking, "Did anyone pick up white kitchen bags? We need the tall white kitchen bags." Now she is guilt-ridden over Will, her eyes darting and constantly rerunning everything in her mind. So, with her teetering on an edge none of us can completely comprehend, we're afraid to even talk about anything in front of her.

Leaning over the railing of the fourth floor I'm getting dizzy and Peter's faith is wavering. What a filthy trick for God to play on us is the gist of it.

"Even if there is a God, I'm not talking to him anymore," he says. "If I've got something to say I'm going to pray to those two guys, if anybody."

"You're bypassing God?" I ask.

"I'm bypassing God," he confirms.

It amazes me that this is having the opposite effect on me. For the first time, I am being drawn to the idea of a superior being.

I, possibly hypocritically, have been looking at this whole thing as if it may be my sign. People who have knocked me for not being a true believer have always said, "One day there will be a sign, there will be no denying it and your doubts will be erased forever. You will never be the same."

I have been staring at this as if it is my sign and I have yet to apply doubt.

In the past couple of days when curious strangers hear about two family members both dying together they assume it was a car crash or something, not two separate deaths miles away from each other.

When we explain the circumstances they say, "There must be some reason," and then walk away without helping us look for it.

In my search, I have pictured Will in the last days at hospice, especially the one night he was there until 3 A.M. "just talking to Dad." He always had so much to say to him. So much praise, so much good, so much gratitude.

"The reason," I begin telling people, "is that while God was checking on my father in those last few days he kept running into Will and he saw the bond between father and son, the unconditional love, the sincerity both spoken and unspoken, and he took such a liking to Will that he decided to take him, too."

It became my little fable, one I would not question for

the time being. One I would use in conversation on my way to making new friends, hopefully twelve in forty-eight hours.

Introspective stops in a stairwell or at Kinko's or in front of a convenience store become the norm for Peter and me as we continue on the errands of death.

Danny has returned to work, taking his pain with him, and Chris has gone home, waiting for the next knock on the door, while we buzz around this heap of responsibilities.

We are openly thankful for the fact that death keeps you so busy. At a time like this it's nice to have no time. Last night, when I was flipping through channels on the TV, I came across that nostalgia network that had been on in my father's hospital room. *Bonanza* was on so I stopped for a minute, and I found that if you only watch *Bonanza* for one minute it is a very profound show. The scene I caught was a silent one. All the boys are circled around Hoss, consoling him with pats on the back and arms around the shoulders. He is sitting there like a boulder and you know it's because before the last commercial break they just killed off the one woman he loved and there is no way he can carry on. But then Pa walks over and says, "Hoss, there's plenty to do."

It is so true. The priest wants a meeting, flowers have to be ordered, photos have to be copied, wills have to be faxed to attorneys, relatives have to be notified.

Making these calls is surreal. Any friends my parents still have are elderly and probably ailing, too. I keep questioning myself before picking up the phone. What kind of shape are they going to be in when I call? Are they even going to be able to hear me?

When I finally start making contact I am astounded at the responses to my father's death. "What can I say, we're shocked, Terry." How they can be shocked when everybody's pushing eighty is beyond me, but I find it heartwarming.

When people ask for details I find myself imitating Peter and cursing out the Coumadin and how doctors shouldn't be prescribing it and how it killed him and . . .

"Oh, my wife's on that," one of my father's close cousins says, stopping me in my tracks.

"Aaa, well, you know, it works fine for most people, it's just, you know . . ."

But then comes the hard part. After I give them directions to the funeral home and times for the viewing and all, how do I throw Will into the mix? I have to tell them. Open or closed, they're going to see the other box there and be a bit curious.

As they go on and on about their fond memories of my father, I keep waiting for a pause in the conversation . . .

Oh, by the way . . .

Aaa, there's something else you need to know . . .

Do you recall my brother Will . . . ?

You might remember him as Bill . . .

I hate to tell you but we've had another tragedy in the fam . . .

Somehow it comes out, and they seem to go along with it. "Geez, I'm sorry to hear that . . ." but then it starts to sink in. "Are you saying this happened yesterday? Both of them died in . . ."

And it just snowballs from there and usually ends with my little fable. "Yes, there must be some reason," they say.

As we go from place to place the pity we receive starts to wear on me. I begin to beg Peter not to tell people. "Just say we're making arrangements for our father," I say. "Leave part two out of it."

When we catch the travel agent at her desk eating lunch she is not thrilled to see us. An out-of-town friend of hers is outside and she was going to take a few minutes and walk over to TCBY with her. And once we tell her our situation—we can get a flight to Arlington for our father's burial service but we can't get back because it's some kind of holiday weekend—she doesn't change her sour expression but agrees to help us and grudgingly starts hitting her keyboard.

"Presidents' Day," she says.

"What?"

"The holiday, it's Presidents' Day."

"Yeah, right," I say, staring off into space.

"Booked, booked, booked," she says, tapping at the keys.

The agency is paneled with posters of all-inclusive resorts with the same type of dark-skinned, long-black-haired women—Ban de Soleil women—all sitting in the only chair on a deserted beach, yellow drink in hand and red hats tilted toward the sun.

Customers keep coming in to see if they've been upgraded on their cruises. "Have I been upgraded yet?" asks a short chubby woman who seems to hug herself as she comes strolling up to the desk.

"Not yet."

"That's OK," she says happily. "I'll check back."

"Is that common?" I ask the travel agent.

"What?"

"Being upgraded when you go on a cruise?"

"Yes," she says, without looking up. "Passengers are always being upgraded."

I go outside to use the pay phone to try and call Jill. She said if there is anything—"absolutely anything"—she can do, to let her know immediately, and we are about to take her up on it. If we're all going to Arlington someone needs to baby-sit Mom, who at the thought of traveling only says, "I can't."

I leave a message and then stop in my tracks when I reenter the travel agency. A funny thing seems to have happened while I was on my way to the pay phone and back. When I return the travel agent is holding Peter's hand, making calls with the other, and hitting the space bar on the computer with her elbows.

"You told her, didn't you?" I shake my head.

Later, while standing outside a pizza place on Singer Island where we are mesmerized by two retired guys who have dressed up their three-wheel senior-citizen scooters like Harleys with black and red metallic paint and faux chrome, we share another moment of insight. After the travel agency experience, we realize that one death in the family really doesn't get you much sympathy in America anymore.

But two, that's where it's at.

View This

Both lids are up.

I should have known the funeral director would forget that little detail. You can't get good help in funeral homes any more than you can in Kmart.

Dan and Peter start to go in but I take root in the lobby or the vestibule or waiting area . . . I don't know . . . to me it is the place where the spooky Victorian furniture screams that there are dead bodies just around the corner but you can't see them from here—that area.

I sit down in a cushioned high-backed chair with arms that curve out like eels, and I begin to shudder from the wails when Danny goes into the viewing room. He has told me how he has dropped to a heap in the shower several times, his gush of tears racing the water bouncing off his back to the drain. "I don't know when it's going to happen and I have no control over it," he says.

I don't know what to say other than, "I know, I know." Even though I really don't. Physically, my grief has been stifled since the first minutes of hearing about Will's accident. After the initial gush of tears and mucus running from my nose onto the phone and my hands and making the first blabbering calls of notification to my brothers I have become stoic. I do not know why.

Peter follows Danny into the room and I assume he will comfort him, but the wailing seems to triple.

I rise up from my chair but then I retreat. I rise again, I retreat again. "I want to help them but they've got both lids up," I tell Christine. "I can't . . . I . . ."

What I never see can't haunt me, can't illustrate my nightmares, I keep telling myself.

My mother has just begun to need to talk about finding Will crumpled over the side of the bathtub. "I touched his face," she says. I can't imagine what images she has shooting through her brain. I want none of that.

I will take my last physical image of him: sitting at my father's desk outside his bedroom writing me a new down-payment check for the funeral home. The day before we had crossed paths and he'd left a check for me in a drawer at hospice. It was supposed to be for $800. He made it out for $8,000.

Now I see him with a big, silly grin, writing out the new check. He's giggling.

"I think I'm having trouble focusing." He laughs. "I've gotta watch those zeros. I just sent out the Florida Power & Light bill. I hope I didn't give them ten thousand dollars."

I will take that goofiness any day over the corpse in the box. "But it helps give you closure," people tell me. I have heard psychologists say that if you don't see someone dead you will always have the feeling that he is still alive, that he might walk through the door any second. Is that supposed to be disturbing, that I may deceive myself into thinking that my father and brother may be out there eating cheese Whoppers, catching a Heat game, having Mexican beers at TGIFriday's, sitting on the patio watching the masts of the sailboats glide through an open drawbridge on a bright blue Sunday morning?

Screw closure. I will take a hundred years of expecting them to come through the door any second over this crap.

My mother wants nothing to do with it at all, though I must say, she doesn't want anything to do with anything right now. The two most crucial people in her life instantly gone. "I don't understand why this is happening," she says. "I don't think I want to live anymore. I just want to go, too."

And I have no argument for her. At the lowest points I have felt the same myself. We all have. "Someone just run me over with a truck," Peter said.

When we were making plane reservations they wanted to see if they could split the family up and put us on separate flights but we said no way. We're all going down together. We were more worried about being the survivors and having to deal with the others' funeral arrangements than anything else.

But this kind of gathering with friends and family and the bodies of the deceased is nice, I guess, in a fucked-up, morbid sort of way.

Our cousin Jill is signing the register, and I recognize her by adding time, just as those new computer imaging programs are capable of doing. I take in her age and the fact that she is now working at a Catholic college where many of the instructors are nuns and she's taken on a sisterly look herself: a pageboy haircut, flat shoes, midcalf skirt, oversized handbag. It's a nun out of the habit and heading for the mall look.

"I'm Terry," I say, since we've only spoken on the phone since this began.

"I know. You dress just like Jack did," she says, referring to her deceased brother. "The exact same kind of sport coat even. It's amazing."

I don't have the heart to tell her that I borrowed the olive tweed jacket a half hour ago from a guy named Steve, but it's nice to think of Jack anyway. He was the older cousin, who on holidays spent a lot of time with us in our aunt's basement, shooting pool and making wisecracks we didn't expect from adults. Jill always seemed to be sitting on a couch upstairs with a Princeton-looking boyfriend whom she would slip out with early.

As she slips into the viewing room I feel obligated to

show her the way, and as other long-lost relatives arrive I try to take on the role of host, like that guy in the outer room at Disney's Haunted Mansion who cordially invites everyone in.

After they shut Will down I stroll around the main viewing room. I stay about twenty paces from my father's box at all times and purposely don't wear my glasses so when I accidentally look his way it's just a blurry airbrushed sort of Dad. With no mustache.

Since it's closed I spend most of my time near Will's casket. "Not bad for a rental," I say, knocking on the hard wood, which clashes with my father's sleek gunmetal model but Will got a flag after all so they're somewhat color coordinated.

My brother Chris walks over and we just stand there between the boxes like cardboard cutouts advertising grief. We don't know what to do with ourselves.

I move on to dawdle by the flower arrangements sent by employers and out-of-state relatives. Peter's company sent two. One from the sales department and one from the business department. I think of that as an extraordinary gesture at first but then I'm reminded that we're dealing in twos. I've even had people come up to me with condolences who say, "I'm sorry about your double tragedy," or "I was so saddened by your pair of losses."

We are no longer a full house.

After the initial stop by the caskets, friends and relatives just sort of turn their backs to them and start talking as if they're at a cocktail party, which is kind of cool.

Somehow, the chitchat among the older folks turns to drunk-driving stories from yesteryear and everyone is trying to top the other. The older generation has some great drunk-driving stories. I especially like the one a cousin tells about his cousin getting pulled over at four in the morning and when the cop asks him if he's been drinking he says, "What the hell else would I be doing out at four in the morning?"

He let him go.

Between the DUI tales the most stunning details about my father and Will come out in passing.

Talking about the war, someone mentions the plate in my father's head.

Plate in his head? That's news to us. Dad never mentioned he had a plate in his head.

"Are you sure?"

"Oh, yes, everyone knew Danny Shine had a plate in his head."

Maybe we don't know as much about this guy as we thought.

"Was he ever a coal miner?" I ask.

Peter pulls me aside and tells me a story Will had told him the night he died. It was during his time in Thailand and he was on a weekend pass in a supposedly safe area when he and his friends were ambushed. Shots were fired and as things escalated they all had to split up and head into the brush. Knowing the bandits were only interested in the American, Will eventually tossed his M-16 off to his Asian girlfriend and sent her into the hills to hopefully save herself.

I knew Will had a dreary job of loading bombs eighteen hours a day but I had no idea he had to always be armed, even during his off time, due to the constant danger of bandits and guerrillas near the base. Luckily, after dark, he was able to come out of cover and zigzag back to the base without incident. But when he returned to a shack in the hills they were to meet at, it was abandoned and there was no sign his girlfriend had ever made it there.

"He never saw her again," Peter says. "He was thinking about going back now. He said, 'Maybe there is a chance she's still alive.' "

I can't believe he would ever go back there.

"Her name was Kiki," Peter says.

Could that be what the brick was for? To go back for a love he lost a lifetime ago?

Later, my mother discloses the fact that the recent name change from Bill to Will was not done on a whim, but rather as a nod to history. A relative who fought in Custer's last stand went by Will Brady and my own mother's father, the mayor of Brooklyn, went by "Will."

Will thought about his name. He thought it was important.

People are lingering. I'm playing DJ, mixing Dad's and

Will's music, fluctuating from Sinatra to Dylan, from "Fly Me to the Moon" to "Tangled Up in Blue."

"It's not working," my wife says of the mix.

"What is these days?" I say. "What is?"

The Irish priest whisks in as if he is the first performer to take the stage at the beginning of Act II, someone with a presence that demands attention, a voice that will cut through the chatter and force people back to their seats.

He has all of these powers, and this *is* Act II. We chose to have two viewings because it seemed to make sense at the time—an afternoon and an evening, oh yeah—but in the evening no one shows up. The elderly don't drive at night, I guess. So it is only us, forced to remain here like the hosts of a gathering after the guests have left. Only we can't just clean up and go to bed. We are obligated to stay.

But the priest breaks our obligation; he takes control with his flowing cassock, colorful scarfs, and perfect Irish brogue.

"Ahh, what you must be going through. The boys . . ." he says, waving his hand over us as we squeeze into the pews, "and Marjorie your mother, to lose her love and her child so close together.

"But let's not talk about suing . . ."

What?

I was so wrapped up in the stereo equipment and playing DJ I wasn't aware that Peter had cornered the priest in the outside waiting room with a tirade about his wavering faith and, more than anything, that the doctors had done my father in by prescribing Coumadin for his heart ailment. The details are fuzzy, but he must have been having a legal consultation with the priest, brazen son of a bitch that he is.

Anyway, it's a great opening, gets everyone's attention. Even Danny's morbid expression changes.

"Suing and hospitals and doctors . . . we are beyond that now. There is no satisfaction to be found there, my sons."

And before you can say, "Yeah, that's easy for you to say," he's describing his own father's demise. A man in his eighties who didn't speak much English and relied on the bus system for transportation. One day in Miami he cut his tongue open but because of the difficulty with the language or reasons unknown several hospitals refused to treat him and sent him on the bus to other facilities around the city until he eventually bled to death.

"Why this happened . . . Why, why, why . . . we do not know," he says, putting his fingertips together. "Doctors, lawyers, hospitals . . . No, we will find no answers there.

"Would you like me to sing some Irish songs at your father's service tomorrow?" he asks.

Yes. Yes we would.

Crashing

I don't remember where I sat.

"Well, it wasn't next to me," my wife says angrily.

At first it seems so petty. We are only a couple of hours from the viewing, and she is harassing me while I stare blankly at the television. Every word pokes me.

"You kept walking away from me," she says of my behavior at the wake.

"What? What are you talking about?"

"People don't act that way at—"

"Act? How do you act? I don't know how the hell to act at something like that. What are you talking about?" I shout, my fingers clawing into the couch. "This is the worst day of my life, how the fuck am I supposed to know how to act?"

I am up and fleeing—"How can you talk to me like this. I would never talk to you like this if it happened to you."—and she is chasing me until I dive into the bed and I am churning and wailing into the comforter, losing myself in the print of the tiny starlike flowers that I never paid attention to before but now my eyelashes sweep across them; they are all I can see and then my teeth are digging into their colors, my mouth is clenched around the fabric, and I tumble onto the floor screeching like an animal that suddenly finds itself under the tires of a speeding car.

I am here. I am not accepting it but I am with it now. I am with Danny dropping to the bottom of the shower stall. I am with Peter, who has taken to lying atop Will's bed and asking for a sign—tell us what happened? How did you just fall? Show me something! I am with Chris as he retreats to his apartment to sit alone. As fragmented and as broken as they all are at this point—I am with them now.

I am with my wife, who couldn't let me keep drifting away. "I love you," she says. "You have to use the people who love you."

What a thought. To know when to use the people who love you.

After that first day of getting the news from the police I thought I had done my grieving right then and there, alone at my desk—sobbing, mucus glistening off my hands—but that was only the initial shock. I had no idea how deep that blood going down the drain traveled.

The music, the time stolen to tend to the arrangements, the responsibility; it's all just froth on a fancy cup of hot coffee. It's not until you blow that fluff away that you can burn yourself on the taste of it all, ball yourself up and go down in flames.

Christine knew that my avoidance, my skittering from one person to the next at the wake, was the same as my not wanting to lean over an open casket.

I explain to her that in my own way I have been going to her. At night, when I cannot sleep I find that all I need to do is place a finger on her body and it somehow calms me until I drift off.

"Oooo, don't touch me while I'm sleeping," she says. "You know I hate that."

Feeling a bit lighter, I get off the floor and go to my son, who was alarmed by the whole outburst. I start to try to explain to him what I'm feeling but there is nothing more horrifying than this kind of emotion in the human voice— the cracking, the quavering that you can't control when you just want to string two damned sentences together.

"Dad," he says, stopping me. "I don't like it when you talk in that voice."

"OK," I mutter, leaving him with only a hug. I will try again and again but I don't know if the inflection strapped to the words of this day can ever change, nor perhaps would I want them to.

It is early but I go back to my bed. It is flat and calming, nothing like the turbulent sea I experienced only a half hour ago. As I bend over and flop down, I close my eyes and start to see spots and shapes as one does when they are lightheaded or get up or sit down too quickly. I lie motionless, listen to my own breathing and watch the shapes shoot by me like an abstract meteor shower. Something large floats up from the distance, entering at its own pace. Then it is before me, like a chiseled bust, revealing only the shoulders and face.

It is my brother Will.

That Other Bible

At the church in North Palm Beach Danny spots three strangers coming across the parking lot. "Who are *they*?" he says.

They're acquaintances, guys from work. They're pall-bearers.

"They look like ZZ Top," someone says.

I'm just happy to see they're not wearing those Home Depot–style Velcro back braces over their suits for the heavy lifting.

We all shuffle around outside the church, wondering how our motorcade looked from afar. "I wish Danny's Ford Escort wasn't the lead car," I say.

All of our funeral home buddies have their game-day faces on, very dignified, almost humanlike outdoors. They nonchalantly swing open the tailgates of the hearses with the same familiarity and ease as my father did on the Ford Country Squire.

The lead man nods to me to gather my pallbearers and starts lining us up to slide the caskets onto rolling gurneys. It becomes awkward because the director has obviously exaggerated how many hands we actually need. People are crowding, squeezing in around both sides. All I've talked about the past couple of days is how we've got to have enough pallbearers. Even Oswald had volunteers. "Oswald's family didn't have to call in the Knights of Columbus," I barked at everyone I knew.

They certainly heeded my call but now the turnout has become cumbersome. Shoulders are bumping, shoes are getting stepped on, people are jogging around the end because they think they see an opening on the other side. I don't want to exclude any family members from getting a hand in *but gee*ʒ*e*, I had these guys drive the fifty miles up from Fort Lauderdale.

Eventually, some people step off. One of the commuter pallbearers has retreated about ten steps back and is standing there in a regal navy blue suit, his hands folded before him, like an executive who's just missed the train from Bayshore to Manhattan.

"You can get the next one," I mutter under my breath.

The inside of the spacious church looks great but it is too cavernous and we are too few for it to wholly embrace us. Flags have been removed from the caskets and replaced with holy shrouds. Jill is sitting off by herself, praying.

I sit with my wife and children, behind my brothers, who are spread out across the front row, evenly spaced and as still as the faux pillars decorating the entranceway of a museum.

There is an elderly gentleman sitting in the back of the church, his hat in his lap, and I keep turning around because no one recognized him earlier when we were outside the church. "Do we know him? Is he just some stranger who attends funerals?" I wondered.

We were about to approach him when we were summoned to carry in the load, but now I don't want to know. I want him to be a stranger. Everybody should have a stranger represented at his funeral, I decide. After all, strangers play the biggest part in our lives.

All of the flowers that were at the wake, horsetrack-winner's-circle-type displays, now adorn the base of the altar. So that's what the flower car was for.

The organ is cranking and I am hoping for "Blowing in the Wind" but gladly settle for "When Irish Eyes Are Smiling," which sways through the air like a field of green.

During the sermon we are mentally in and out. The priest's accent is great, and whenever he takes a personal slant our ears perk up. We cling to the mention of our names, to the details of them both serving their country in the armed services, to the sympathy for our mother who cannot yet envision a future that she would want to participate in.

"Oh, Marjorie, what a lovely lady in so much pain," he says, spreading his arms to the roof. "Lord, you have taken so much from her."

Big sloppy chords on the keyboard take us through moments of meditation but then the Mass turns to formality and our priest seems more like a deity than the personable chap who graced us with his presence at the viewing. As the service winds down we realize he isn't going to sing any Irish songs. Maybe he forgot, maybe his throat is dry, maybe he has a wedding at three and is saving himself—who knows.

Later, when we take a few people over to TGIFriday's for potato skins and beer served in plastic boots for some promotion, the loss of the songs is in the air.

"What happened to the Irish songs?" I say. "The Gaelic singing he promised."

"I know, what was that all about?" Peter says. "Did he just blow it off?"

"He's all accent." I laugh.

"What happened to the songs?" someone at the end of the table laments.

"All accent, no action," I say in a toast. "You can't get good help these days, not even in churches."

Amen.

"Thank God for the organist," I say.

And right now the organist is still swirling around us as the Mass creeps to a close.

This is only a stopping point for my father, he still has the hero's welcome and the twenty-one-gun salute and all at Arlington to come. But it is the end of the road for my brother so I told the priest I would like to say a few words and read something for Will.

While tangled in my thoughts about God, it is strange for me to step up to the pulpit, a crucifix high above my head.

"All Will ever cared about was other people," I say.

"And I think that's part of the reason why he's not sitting out there today. Between helping my father, my mother, and me and my brothers, it sapped him just enough to make him vulnerable."

Will wore the world like a wetsuit, tightly against his skin; he felt everything.

I tell them how Will saw my fatigue and recommended the burgers, a twelve-pack, a chair, and everything would be all right.

"And it was," I say.

"For a little while."

My voice is beginning to tremble but I try to hold it still for Dante, who is glaring up at me.

"I want to read something for Will from that other bible," I say, holding up a fat book of the complete works of Bob Dylan. I am desperate to put the music that has always been my savior together with my newfound faith in the existence of God, even if it is only fleeting. Even if it only buys me a day of peace.

At the end of his life, I didn't know where Will stood on religion or if his disgust with the service had ever subsided. But I knew he was still listening to Bob Dylan. In fact, on his nightstand I had found he'd written down the words to a recent song: "It's not dark yet, but it's getting there." And I knew if it hadn't been for an older brother like him someone like me might have gone through life ignorant of the value of such music. I could easily have become one of those "How can you stand that voice? I can't understand a word he's saying" people.

I understand that voice as I read a passage from "Restless Farewell" that refers to the false clock that marks our time and includes the lines "And if I see the day/I'd only have to stay/So I'll bid farewell in the night and be gone."

When I finish I look down at the faces of my brothers. Through all of this we have talked about how much we have loved our parents but we've yet to take a moment to express our feeling for one another.

"I love you, Danny, I love you, Chris, I love you, Peter," I say, and when I turn to the box I am glad that his body, even if only a shell, is there at my feet.

"I love you, Will."

Buschwhacked

The night Will left this world there was one empty Busch beer can on his nightstand and exactly four left in the twelve-pack carton in the fridge.

One for each remaining brother we have decided, grasping for significance.

"Can you believe he left us each one?" Peter marveled at the discovery.

Many conversations would ensue as to when the Busches should be lifted and drained. With something this important we didn't want to just do it on a whim; these were serious beers.

We have to have the perfect moment.

"Now," Peter says after the funeral.

Everyone is just milling around the condo while my mother naps so it *would* be the perfect time but . . .

But there have been other perfect times and in each

instance the bottom has fallen out. We never seem to be able to pull it off. The excuses are rampant: "It's too early." "I need to eat something first." "Can't we wait until after my favorite TV show is over?"

"I hate Busch," I said, putting an end to one opportunity.

I am sitting out on the balcony in a plastic chair, watching a straight line of lightly pigmented birds cut across the sky before looping around and clasping together like a charm bracelet, when Peter decides to return to the mission, a gleam in his eye.

"Chris, you ready?" he asks.

"Yeah, sure."

"Danny—don't go anywhere," Peter says, heading into the kitchen.

In seconds he is standing in the living room, the cardboard container slung at his waist, his hand hooked into the dispensing hole.

He swings it up and pops one out.

"I should really be getting Daniel home," Danny says.

"I don't think so," Chris says, looking away. "Maybe later."

"There's not going to be any later," Peter says, getting pissed off. "We're all together now. Who knows what's going to happen later? It's not about the perfect moment anymore. It's about everybody being in the same room at the same time."

With no takers, Peter disgustedly heads back to the kitchen, the cardboard beer carrier dangling off him like a broken appendage, and I can hear him say into the refrigerator: "When this is all over, we'll never be together again."

Brainstorm

Danny phones me at home and, without so much as a hello, states that he thinks Will should be buried at Arlington, too.

I assume he has just gotten up off the floor of his shower, scraped the tile scum off the back of his thighs, and called me in a moment of delirium.

Since the funeral director brought it up we kind of looked into Will's military background and as far as we could tell he was . . . discharged. But we couldn't find anything about honorable or dishonorable, just that he was discharged.

Raised on my father's war stories, Will joined the air force as an act of emulation but the contrasts of their experiences in the service were extreme. For Dad, it was the highlight of his life; for Will, I believe it was an obvious disaster. He didn't say much but based on the tidbits he released—incompetent superiors running the base in Thailand like a fast-food restaurant, eighteen-hour days of breathing jet fumes from constantly idling planes, loading bombs nonstop during a supposed cease-fire—he found no honor in serving his country.

One assessment we found from a commanding officer took note of what I think he called Will's "remarkable negativity." If Will was to receive any commendations during his tour of duty it would not have been for his heroics in the face of profound adversity but rather for something like his extraordinarily bad attitude under extreme conditions.

We are very proud of both of our soldiers, each taking the right stand at the right time in history, but Will in Arlington . . .

Maybe Danny is thinking since Will is being cremated and wouldn't really take up much of their precious space, they wouldn't care about his record or whatever. But . . .

"I mean put him right in with Dad," he says.

Yes, what a brainstorm. Nestle him right in there, tucked like a football in my father's arms.

It goes right back to the opportunity thing that Peter had brought up. Will could never have imagined going off to eternity in a parade while his father holds him in his arms. Forget what he thought of the military, he would eat up the fact that, in the end, those bastards would be sending him off with full honors: a wondrous discharge.

What would be the channels to pull this off? I am leery of checking with Arlington. I already made a fool of myself when I tried to arrange things with them while Dad was still in hospice. I was so caught up in getting everything set up ahead of time that I kept insisting that they were being unreasonable for not being able to tell me exactly what day he could be buried and what time we'd have to be there and . . .

"Sir, he has to die first," the nice woman said.

"Oh, right, right," I stammered. "I'm sorry . . . we've got so much to do we're just getting ahead of ourselves. I'm sorry . . . I'm sorry."

"That's quite all right," she said.

"Why do we have to ask anybody?" Danny asks.

"You mean just put him in there," I say.

It was only about a week ago that I had read an article about Clinton getting into trouble for allowing relatives of a family that had done some favors for him to be buried in Arlington National Cemetery who did not meet the qualifications.

"They made them dig up the bodies," I tell Danny.

"They dug up the bodies."

"Yeah, they had to move them."

I envision some summer day two years from now, military police surrounding the grave site as the casket is raised and the top is popped. A member of the family would have to be there and something tells me it would be me.

"Get William Joseph Shine out of there," the federal investigator would say.

"Lieutenant Shine won't let go, sir. I can't get the urn out of his hands. He's clutching it like a football."

"Pry it from his fingers, soldier!"

"What the hell," I tell Danny. "It's final, we've got to do it."

Life Jackets

We are zooming down Federal Highway, between errands, when I say to Peter, "We should take him for a beer."

A few minutes ago we had to drop off a key to Mom's condo with a nun who used to work with Jill. Jill isn't coming down until Thursday afternoon, a couple of hours after we fly to Washington, D.C., so she wanted to have a key in case Mom is sleeping when she arrives.

The sister operates a small tutoring school to combat illiteracy in the community and for some reason Jill had told us to act as if we were really interested in her cause when we stopped by. We asked her for a tour and she seemed thrilled as she took us around a maze of several small rooms.

"This used to be a doctor's office," she said. "That's why some of the rooms are so tiny."

"Oh, yeah, it's all those little rooms they stick you in," I said, peeking into one that had been turned into a miniature library.

She pointed out some computers that were donated. "Have to have computers these days," she said.

"Yes you do," Peter agreed.

After we got in the car and scooted away we talked

about who acted more interested. "My interest was genuine," I said. "You were acting."

"No," Peter disagreed. "I was very interested. You were putting on a show."

In the end we decided that we were behind her and would make a sizable donation after all of this was over. "With Mom's money?" I asked.

"I don't know," Peter said.

"With Will's money?" I said.

"Maybe."

"We should take him for a beer."

The funeral home is only about a quarter mile up on the right and the parking lot is deserted, as it usually is this time of day. But I have no fear of entering anymore.

"Where are we going to take him?" Peter says, rubbing his hands together. "They have some nice bars on the water around here."

We pull right up under the overhang by the front door and walk right through the heavy doors. We are home.

Les, a tall character, comes lilting down the hallway, and in a voice caught somewhere between reverential and can't I even eat my lunch without being bothered, he says, "How are you gentlemen today?"

As the distance between us closes he sees the familiar faces and releases an earnest sigh. "Ahhh, how are you holding up?"

"We're holding up," I say. "Is Will still on the premises? They didn't ship him off yet, did they?"

"No, no, he should still be here."

"Could we see him?"

"Sure, let me check in the back."

As he floats back toward us he is holding the urn up above his shoulder. He is a tall man, and the method in which he is carrying it reminds me of the way young kings were carried through town in Egyptian times.

Shifting to cradle it in front of him, he faces the gold plaque attached to the pine in our direction. What little light this hallway offers shines off the metal and we are charmed once again by the WILL inscribed beneath his full name.

"We'd like to take him out for a drink," I blurt.

"What??" Les says, immediately taking one giant step backward, and then another, and then another.

The urn is high above his shoulder again and we start to pursue him, to give chase. After all, there are two of us, and if we can't wrestle our brother away from an unsuspecting mortician who hasn't even had a chance to eat lunch yet then we are not the men we propose to be.

He's quick though, so I pull out the ace in the family hole. "Actually it's our mom who wants to see him. You know she's not well," I say. "We're just going to run him over to the condo and head back. All right?"

"Give me a minute," he says.

When he returns he's got Will all dressed up in one of those velour bags, similar to the ones that bottles of Crown

Royal come in. "This is best if you're going to be traveling with him," he says.

I tighten up the drawstring, we buckle him up to a seat belt in the back of my Isuzu, and we're off.

There is no better time to be in Florida than early February, the A/C replaced by cool breezes, the sun more gallant than daunting. We pull into a waterway café that has a bar out back that we could see from the other side of the Intracoastal. I lug Will through the dining room where couples are scattered about, hammering the crab shells of a late lunch. The parcel feels good in my arms and the burst of water and light when we step out toward the bar that sits at the end of a short pier makes my eyes widen instead of squint.

There are only a few patrons around the circular bar so Will gets his own stool between us. We are chagrined when the bartender says: "No Busch."

But we settle for three Budweisers, which Will probably would have preferred anyway if he wasn't such a cheapskate.

I look up and there is a ring of life preservers attached to the entire perimeter of the thatched roof covering the bar. "This is a floating bar," the bartender says. "We have to have one life jacket for everyone at the bar. It's a regulation."

My head spins at the old-style orange life vests, and Peter and I shift our seating to face the drawbridge where the Jet Skis shoot under like devilish mice and the large charter boats demand traffic be stopped and steel grates hoisted to allow for their monstrous third and fourth levels.

We are envious of both on a beautiful day like this. I loosen the drawstring on Will's jacket and the bartender peers over the edge of the bar. "Oh, that's what you've got down there."

A what? A who? A where are we at this point? I do not know.

We feebly talk about how Will would have enjoyed this place. "Life preservers for everybody at the bar, I love it," I can hear him saying.

We order another three beers and stare across to the other side of the narrow Intracoastal, where another water-side restaurant sits, another dockside bar, another lunch crowd, another view.

"Her name was Kiki?" I ask Peter.

"Yeah," he says. "I really think he was going to go back and search for her, even after all this time."

"I believe you are right," I say.

I look down at Will sitting between us, his own stool, his own Bud, and I know an hour will easily pass with us talking about what a pissa he was. This is supposed to be our healthy little way of saying good-bye, but who are we fooling?

As our beers empty, his are backing up and sweating in this glorious sunshine in a way that only reminds us that our brother, who was only a phone call away three days ago, is now just a pile of fried bones and ash.

A Second Dog?

Up and down, inside and outside, sideways and high-ways, and it's hard to know when you're stationary. The emotions keep changing and rearranging themselves and it's impossible to focus on today.

But suddenly I'm home and it seems like I've been away for months. We're in the bedroom packing for the plane to D.C. and I hear rustling in the living room at the other end of the house, sounds like someone is remodeling.

We've had a houseguest for weeks but I've forgotten all about him since I've been so preoccupied with tragedy. This is the short of it: My daughter went out with a group of friends to a movie one night a couple of months ago and when I went to pick them up one of the guys stayed at the shopping center. I figured he was going to get a burger or something but a couple of hours later I ask my daughter who she's talking to on the phone and she says it's that guy, he's still at the shopping center.

"Why didn't he have me give him a ride home?" I said.

"He doesn't have a home to go home to," Brynn said.

"Are you dating a homeless guy?" I asked.

Anyway, one thing led to another and we decided to let him stay with us for a while and immediately little things began trickling out about how he can't get along with his stepdad and he's been in jail.

"He's been in jail?"

"Twice."

But he hasn't been in a hell of a lot of trouble except for . . . you know those itty-bitty screens that go in the end of faucets to keep the stream of water under control? He stripped them out of several spouts in the house, so when you go to wash your hands your entire shirt gets soaked. He needed the screens for his pot pipe.

"I'm going to replace the ones in the sinks," he told me. "I promise. As soon as I get a job."

But he never did and I've been so caught up with everything I haven't even had the strength to kick him out and now here I am about to travel and I'm going to have an ex-con watching my house.

I go out in the living room and he has dragged our good dining room chairs several feet from the table and he is hovering between two of them doing some kind of jail-yard pull-ups right there in my home.

"This isn't a fucking prison yard," I yell at him. "You don't do your twenty minutes a day of allotted exercise in my living room."

Damn it, I've got to pack. I don't need this. "Let me just kick him out now," I say to Christine.

"He'll be OK. Besides, we need someone to feed the animals," she says, reminding me that we have a second dog now.

The second dog we didn't have months ago. My family snuck it in on me while I was occupied, tending to the ill.

I remember coming home in the evening and just shaking my head as my wife told me he was climbing the fence and digging these enormous holes along the side of the house. "Of course he is. There is no reason for a second dog," I said. "The first dog has all the responsibility of watching the house and barking at fire; that frees the second dog up to do whatever he pleases, to wreak havoc."

Something is liberating about this feeling I'm having here at home. Things are irritating me again and it feels good as I stuff all my clothes into a duffel bag and we all head out to the van.

"Did you make sure everything was locked up?" Christine says.

"We've got a burglar living inside the house," I remind her. "I don't want to lock him in."

All my brothers drive to the airport together in Danny's car and we run into them at check-in and walk single file the length of the terminal to our gate. With my children and little Daniel there are eight of us.

Peter, who is also a single parent, has a four-year-old daughter named Nicole but she has been shielded from all of this, staying with relatives in New York.

We've got about thirty minutes until takeoff and I use the time wisely. I tell a stranger about how I have an ex-con watching my house while we're away and I buy a Mrs. Fields cookie with a hundred-dollar bill.

Little Daniel is staring out the thick slanted windows overlooking the runway and he waves his father over when they start loading the luggage. "There's Grandpa," he says.

And sure enough, there's the encased casket, being whisked across the Tarmac in its own little transport vehicle. We are all flying together. The transport driver jackknifes around, backs up, and swiftly slides the airtray into the belly of the 737.

Up and away.

Whatever You Do, Don't Flush

The shuttle bus takes us from the airport directly to the hotel. "This isn't the kind of neighborhood you want to be walking around," the driver tells us.

The travel agent gave us the option of two Sheratons in D.C. and suggested we pick the closest one since we have to be at Arlington by 8 A.M. the following morning.

The Sheraton a little farther away is the type with glass elevators and whatnot; this is the type with security gates. But they've got a pool on the roof so we take the kids up, not to go swimming but to take a little tour of the place and kill some time. Considering there was only a slight breeze at ground level the forceful wind blowing across the roof is startling. We start spinning around, spreading our wings and letting it blow us across the patio. We whirl and drop like out-of-control kites but continue to get back up again and again. We hurl a single white life preserver up into the turbulence and watch it sputter in each direction before cartwheeling into the pool. Everyone is laughing, our pants are flapping and making a *thwack, thwack* sound similar to the sound of a playing card in the spokes of a bicycle. When we yell at one another the words fly into the back wall and splatter into a million syllables. The wind is beating us up and we can't get enough.

Daniel and Dante eventually fly back toward the stairwell and elevators so we give chase. We stop back at one of the rooms to give Mom a call. Jill is there and everything seems to be going fine. "She gave me a haircut. It looks just like hers," Mom says. "I really like it."

Jill gets on the line to remind us to visit her father's grave site. Her father, former attorney general John Mitchell of Watergate fame, is also buried at Arlington—for being a navy officer during WWII, not for starring in the Watergate scandal.

"I left a pipe on his grave last time I was there," Jill says. "I'm sure they clean up stuff like that, but could you check? I was just wondering if it's still there."

Check for smoking pipe on Mitchell grave, we all make a mental note.

It's only about 3 P.M. and no one wants to be locked in a room with the kids so we head to the lobby to see where else that shuttle goes.

"You can go to the mall," the desk clerk says.

"No thanks," we answer.

There's a bar off the main entrance and if I could go back in time and take back any words I've ever uttered in the past decade or two, it would be these: "I wonder if they have a happy hour and a free buffet?"

No one else seems interested but I persist to the point where I leave them all at the elevator and go to ask the bartender if kids are permitted at the bar.

"Not at the bar, but in the bar's OK," he says.

I excitedly hurry back to catch them before they jump in the elevator. "We're all welcome at the Quarterdeck," I say. "And I think I saw them putting out some triangle sandwiches."

The entire crew trudges behind me and maybe it is the whole happy hour phrase that gets the better of me, or I am understandably and excusably a bit delusional due to our pair of losses, but anyway, the whole downside of bringing a bunch of extremely depressed people to a bar in the middle of the day when there is nothing but hours locked in a hotel and a 6 A.M. cemetery wake-up call lying before them never occurs to me.

"Beer, Chris?" I say, heading toward the bartender.

"No, I don't think so."

"Danny, a beer?"

"Ahh, nah."

"Well, I'm gonna get a beer. You want a soda or something?"

"Oh, you're going to have one?" Chris says. "Sure, I guess I'll have one."

"Yeah, I'll get one too," Danny says, as if to be social.

"What's up? We doing some shots?" Peter says, straggling up the steps to the Quarterdeck.

Things get a little fuzzy from this point on. I remember the turning point being when I saw Danny smoking. I hadn't seen him smoke in twenty years.

"Danny, you're smoking," I yelled to him, and he looked up and lifted his glass in a toast to me.

I do know the buffet turned out to be lame, mostly veggie-platter-type offerings and at some point we bought some potato chips in the gift shop and decided to go back up to the rooms and have everyone cram into one suite for sort of a family night and rent *The Devil's Advocate* starring Al Pacino off the pay-per-view but then I remember us calling down to the front desk and asking if the shuttle could take us for beer.

"No, but we can have a taxi make the run," the clerk said. And then Peter went off in a taxi and returned with Cheez Doodles and beer. While he was away I stuffed washcloths in the drains and filled the sinks with ice to create a couple of makeshift coolers and I recall marveling at Chris when he did this amazing thing with his arms, overlapping both forearms and somehow loading up the space between them with rows of cans, turning himself into a human beer dispenser. When you were ready for another he would come around and one would just pop out.

This wasn't half bad, I thought. Danny's laughing again, Chris has dropped his inhibitions and become the boy I remember, I have stepped above my dry melancholy. We are flushing out our systems, drinking the spirits, allowing for the natural playfulness to surface once again.

Turning point number two came when little Daniel said, "Have you seen my father?"

After we realized both he and the human dispenser had vanished from family night we set out searching the hotel several times, including the bottom of the pool at the top of the hotel.

"Maybe they went to the mall," Peter said.

While we were questioning the bartender someone was stepping out of the men's room and when he cracked the door it sounded like he was leaving a party. I peeked in and this is very vivid in my memory. There they were, arm in arm in a cloud of smoke, standing in front of the row of sinks, staring directly into the mirrors at themselves and singing "Travelin' Man" in a "Row, Row, Row Your Boat" fashion with Danny a step ahead so it sounded something like this: "I'm a trav . . . I'm a man . . . a traveling . . . I'm a –ing man."

Quite soulful.

But it was fast becoming the theme song to a complete breakdown. Somehow a contest to see who could best imitate our Irish priest started up but after it was long over we all still had Irish accents ("Can you snatch me another pint outta the sink there, me laddy?") and couldn't seem to shake them. Even when Danny tried to go into his Al Pacino imitation—which he'd always nailed in the past—

it came out like Al Pacino playing a drunken Irish priest.

"I can't get me regular voice back," Danny said.

"Perhaps this is just the way we're going to talk from now on, 'tis our Irish heritage surfacing," I said. "Let's not fight it."

We all kept drinking and, under the influence of both alcohol and having seen the trees and white stones of Arlington from the windy rooftop, two of us decided to leave the confines of the hotel at around 2 A.M. and start hitchhiking down the parkway and, without naming names, one of us ended up getting picked up by the police while straddling a fifteen-foot fence surrounding a nearby government building. "I thought it was a shortcut to Arlington," he told the officer.

He also told the whole grimy double death story, with an Irish accent I'm sure, and evidently the cop didn't want to arrest the son of a war hero on the eve of his father's burial, because he ended up just stuffing him into the back of the car sans cuffs and unloading him back at the hotel. "This isn't the kind of neighborhood you want to be walking around," he said.

For most of us, morning brings no need for a wake-up call. We are already up and this is turning into one big messy day. Relay showers are being taken, blow-dryers are short-circuiting, people are putting on other people's underwear. Danny and Chris hastily try to make coffee for everybody from a complimentary pot in one of the rooms. Coffee is everywhere, like someone used it for chewing tobacco and then spit it all around the room. Danny hands me a mug.

"Here, you better have some coffee," he says.

I look in the cup and it's nothing but a blob of grinds.

It's a coffee meatball.

The Snap of a Flag

We are in awe of our invitation to Arlington, of our loss equaling this honor.

The odd February sun is strong but the day is still founded in the cold. I finally get to wear the $150 leather jacket that has hung in my Florida closet indefinitely, and it's at my father's funeral.

Peter, who is wearing a dark suit, isn't happy about the way we're dressed. We're all over the place—leather, ski jackets, hiking boots, sneakers. "Maybe they rent trench coats and I can cover you all up when we get there," he says.

The kicker is that before we left Florida he lined up a film company in D.C. to videotape the ceremony for five hundred bucks and I think he forgot that we were all going to be in it.

The limousine we're riding in is stocked with bottles of spring water and everyone starts guzzling away his cotton mouth. "I think they charge for that," Christine says.

Everyone stops guzzling.

Palms extend as Brynn starts passing around those tiny power mints, shaking them out of a small black-and-silver capsule. The miniscule dots are lost in our hands. "Are they invisible?" Chris says, squinting into his cupped fingers.

The guard at the gate salutes us through and everything appears in slow motion as we turn to the rows of evenly erected headstones stretching to the horizon at every turn.

We are led to a central building where we go through sort of a debriefing, meeting the principals: a military chaplain, a civilian priest who also has an Irish accent, and a governmental family liaison who tells us how to get parking passes for when we return to visit the grave site.

"We all get passes, right?" Peter asks.

"You all get passes," he says.

There's a glass-walled waiting area at the front of the building for the family and it is there we meet two gentlemen who have been asked by their parents to attend the service. Their folks were unable to make the trip, so they have been sent as representatives. That is so cool. I wonder if I'll ever be dispatched as a family representative. Anyway, one is the son of a close cousin of my father's and the other is the son of a boyhood friend we'd often heard my father refer to as Punter.

"Where'd he get that name Punter?" we ask.

"He was a punter," the son says.

Such are the mysteries of life.

One of the men is a Georgetown professor and is dressed like an actor playing a Georgetown professor and Punter's kid is built more like a center and with his tight suit and dark shades, he could easily pass for Secret Service.

The video guy shows up and asks if there is anything we don't want included in the shoot. Peter looks at *us* out of the corner of his eye but knows he can't eliminate his own family, though I am sure he's trying to figure out how to put us in the background and give Georgetown and Secret Service more prominence in the film.

"Oh, no, is that the hearse?" Peter says, moving toward the large windows. Everything has been first class up to this point. The funeral home in Florida was immaculate, the church pristine, the caskets polished to perfection, even the limo for the ride over here is no prom job. It is slick and professional.

"Look at it. It looks like something the Blues Brothers would show up in," Peter says, staring at the hearse.

I flash back to being at the conference table with the funeral director that first day when I was alone, and he said something about how we'd have to contract with another funeral home in Washington since there'd be a day before going to Arlington. "That will cost at least twelve hundred dollars," he said. "But wait . . ."

He then left the room to make a call and upon his return he said: "Never mind, I got someone who can do it for four hundred dollars."

Maybe I should have asked, "Why can he do it for four when . . ."

But here is my answer. If it was on one of the checklists

as to whether we wanted (a) A 1998 jet-black Cadillac
Seville hearse, or (b) A 1979 powder blue Buick Skylark
hearse, I certainly would have made the right decision, but
of all the options on all the forms we went through that
was not one of them. I swear.

"What kind of blue is that?" Peter asks for the second
time.

"Powder," I repeat.

The one saving grace is the horses. The liaison explains
to us that the casket will be transferred from the hearse to
the carriage and then there will be about a quarter of a mile
procession. We can either walk behind the caisson or ride
in the limo.

We conjure up images of Princess Di's kids gracefully
following their mother's procession, of John John saluting
in shorty pants, and there is no doubt that we will be hoof-
ing it.

"Who will we be presenting the flag to?" the liaison
asks.

"To Danny," I say. "He's the eldest."

At the transfer location we stop counting how many soldiers have assembled after about fifty. We need this, a tribute of majestic proportions—wintergreen rolling hills and
the Washington Monument in our foreground, aimed like a
missile toward the heavens.

The transfer from the hearse to the carriage is tedious
and regimented as a band plays from a strategic position on
the horizon, its muffled drums demanding attention. Our

eyes focus on the gold stripes running straight up the soldiers' pants legs and the white gloved fingers that inch the flag-draped casket into place.

Being here in the land of heroes and patriots seems to be lifting us above our constant misery. As the horse-drawn carriage rolls and the soldiers' calculated movements of respect unfold before us, they seem to be taking some of the pain away.

Words like duty and honor are not falling on our usually cynical ears. They are elevating our father's memory.

I recall the words of the foolish doctor who enters someone's life in the final stages; runs the tests, checks the charts four minutes a day, and then says something like . . . *Your father just doesn't have what it takes.*

He has no idea.

These men do.

In a time when people are forgotten so easily we have been staggered by the response there has been to our father's death. From his former employer declaring to us, "This corporation would not be what it is today if it weren't for Dan Shine," to a waitress near his home telling us his famously big smile would carry her through a double shift, to this display for a soldier who will not be forgotten, we are not only grateful but will be forever envious.

Earlier in the week, when we started reading cards on the floral arrangements we found remarks like, "You were the greatest," and "You were a prince," and we each admitted that there is not another prince among us. No matter how hard we try, none of us will ever overshadow our father's legacy.

The best I could hope for when I go is for some recognition by association. "Oh, did you hear Terry Shine passed away?"

"Really, I remember his father. He was a great man. A prince."

But that's OK with us.

With our mishmash of clothing we look like refugees at the end of a military parade as we try to walk in sync with the honor guard.

We watch for the salutes to signal the placing of our hands over our hearts. We are absorbing every nuance, soaking in every detail and sound: the click of military shoes on blacktop, the snort of the lead horse, the short barks of the commanding officer.

When they lift the flag up off the casket to prepare for burial, the soldiers on each side hold it flat out and extend it like a net that could catch someone falling from the sky.

It catches us as their grips tighten and the ritual of folding the banner begins. We can almost feel our own hands pulling up the slack.

"Ladies and Gentlemen, this is the flag of the United States of America," the lead soldier announces. "This is the flag of our country—the flag that unites us all."

Step forward and cut it in half . . . shake it out and half again . . . Snap it . . .

"Many Americans—both humble and great—have lived,

202 T. M. Shine

served, and died for the sake of this noble emblem—a symbol of the life we live in freedom and democracy. All soldiers aspire to conduct themselves according to its virtues—DUTY, HONOR, COUNTRY—asking only to be remembered for the sacrifices they have made for the betterment of this land."

Triangle fold, step, triangle again, step, closer and closer, tighter and tighter . . .

"As we honor this flag today, we also pay tribute to the life, legacy, and honorable service of Daniel L. Shine, Second Lieutenant, United States Army."

Tighter, tighter . . . until no red, no blood is showing. Just the bright blue and the glow of the stars.

"May his soul find eternal rest and peace with Almighty God, and may the God in whom we trust continue to bless this majestic land we proudly call the United States of America."

The perfect triangle.

As they lay the flag in Danny's lap we are all trembling, our grips loosened and limp from anything but this end we now stand in.

Daddy, hold on to my brother, I cry to myself.

A plane thrusts up overhead, an unplanned but fitting tribute. Our ears are tuned back to the sounds: the engines roaring, the commander shouting above the rumble, the rifles cracking the morning, the spent casings dropping to the ground. We are listening.

We are sober.

We are proud.

For the moment we are refreshed in the way a smack in the face stands you straight up and awakens you to the significance, the importance, of a particular event.

Our formation is tight and Danny's limp is more pronounced than ever as we quickly march back to the limousine. Our deliberate steps are broken only by the voice of the Irish priest who stops us in an island of sun between two fat branched trees. He wants to offer private condolences, his Irish whisper floating out in bursts of cold white breath. He asks for each of our names individually and then repeats them. Daniel. "Yes, Daniel." Peter. "Yes, Peter." I like the way he says, "Terence."

"Yes, Terence."

He holds us there, his voice racing us toward acceptance. Leaning on allegory he swoops us down through the valley of death and lifts us back up to the currents of the river of life and . . .

"And, Father, speaking of rivers," Danny says. "If I don't find a bathroom in the next thirty seconds I'm gonna . . ."

"Oh, oh, by all means. Well, you have my blessings, Daniel. All of you."

"Geez, how long do you think Danny was waiting for a water reference?" I say to Peter as we hustle back up to the limo.

The driver returns us to the main building and while Danny is pissing a river we check at the main desk about getting a location for the grave of John Mitchell. The attendant, who has an extremely gruff voice, turns to a computer terminal and starts a search. He asks for a middle name but we can't think of one and I realize this might be hopeless since it's a pretty common name.

He starts coughing up middle names—Gregory, Michael, Newton . . .

"Oh, yeah, Newton. How could we forget that," I say.

"John Newton Mitchell," he says, printing out the directions.

The limo winds us through roads that are laid out like a gameboard, Candy Land lanes that meander just because they can, and then we reach a certain point where we can go no farther because the roadway is sealed off with thick black chains, the kind you usually only see on battleships.

We only have the limo reserved for another fifteen minutes, so rather than try to find another way around we jump out, climb over the chains and start jogging up a steep hill. "It's supposed to be near the Tomb of the Unknown Soldier," someone says. "There, that sign is pointing up there for the Unknown Soldier."

The morning has grown some and we are fighting through a throng of tourists who are descending the hill. When we reach the area we split up, everybody taking a different row.

"Hey, look, Lee Marvin," I say.

"Was he a war hero?" Peter says, coming over.

"I don't know, they wouldn't let you in here for just being a hero in movies, would they?"

"What, do you think he's in here for *The Dirty Dozen*?" Danny says.

"Among others."

"Did you ever see *The Big Red One*?"

"*Comancheros* was the best."

"Maybe it's not that Lee Marvin."

"There's a lot of John Mitchells but only one Lee Marvin," I say.

"Lee Marvin is dead?" Chris says.

"We're running out of time," Christine reminds us.

Oh, yeah.

And we haven't got far to run, only about a row away from Lee Marvin we come upon the John Newton Mitchell stone, which is about five times the size of our father's generic stone. "He must have really planned ahead," I say.

What a location. On the top of a hill, Lee Marvin as a neighbor, tourists bustling by, the pant cuffs and black-mirrored shoes of the honor guard at the Tomb of the Unknown Soldier visible through the brush.

Dad's spot is kind of overlooking the freeway ramp, but they say there aren't many plots left here at Arlington. They're going to run out of room long before they run out of heroes, I suppose.

No pipe.

As we return to the limo and drift out of the cemetery I start to observe the individual names on the generic stones. They no longer look like this monotonous row upon row of white caps. I even notice that the lines are not as symmetrical as I thought: some stones are crooked, a little off-kilter, time has settled some deeper, shifted some to the left, tipped some to the right. The stones all seem to be fighting for individuality . . . and winning.

It takes an eternity for the tail end of this long vehicle to pass through the exit gates and I wonder where we are headed now. My mother has a new hairdo and they are gone, gone, gone.

Both humble and great.

Restless Farewell

Oh, if it could end with a parade, with soldiers who had risen at dawn, dressed together and tugged at their sleeves until they were taut and ready for inspection. Oh, if it could end with the lone white-gloved bugler pacing out to the horizon, making a square turn and pursing his cold lips around the simple notes of "Taps."

But it refuses to. The ceiling remains my sky and I can't seem to move beyond this, can't seem to open the days back up.

The condominium is empty. Mom has gone to stay with Danny for a while and I've stopped by to pick up some things. I open the double doors, slide the vase and hat rack over to keep them propped and leave them that way. The A/C is blowing but I open all the windows too. There is no end to the suffocating sensation I feel every time I enter this sanctuary. I guess that's what it is now, this sanctuary of loss.

But it is not as if the sight of their belongings—a glimpse of a toothbrush, a worn leather wallet on a bureau—overwhelms me with memories, because I see my father and Will in everything now, whether I'm in the condo or not. As I've gone about my business this past week they have attached themselves to the most mundane pieces of the day. I can see them in the folds of a paper napkin, in the credits of a TV show, in a garage-sale painting—something will jump out and morph into some kind of reminder of them.

There was a song playing the other afternoon, one I've heard dozens of times, but the lyrics caught me off guard as the singer sang of apparitions that won't leave him alone. He decides he has had enough of the memories of a lost loved one that seem to attack him at every turn—"I chew up and I choke down / The scraps you choose to leave around."

The song is called "Leave" and the writer is haunted by his brother's death but I can never see myself having the guts to say, "Leave." Maybe because it's hard to tell anyone to leave when you feel so abandoned, maybe because a world of apparitions welcomes me, embraces me so sweetly.

I was looking at an old *Life* magazine the other day and a photo of a 1950s movie star sitting in the backseat of a car jolted a vision of my father sitting on the edge of the backseat of a sedan zipping through New York City. He is leaning forward, reaching for the lighter up front to ignite his sister's cigarette. I am ducking out of the way, sliding over to the door to be closer to the skyscrapers and pushing my face against the glass, smudging it with one more memory. It is the only time I ever recall seeing him in the backseat of a car. He must have had a whole life in backseats that I knew nothing about—scurrying to meetings across town, business lunches, friendly tag-alongs with old and new associates—but with me he was always holding on to the steering wheel, always the driver.

"Hey, you know I only saw my father in the backseat of a car once? One time," I shouted to Christine this morning, leaving her to decide if I am going nuts or not. "One time."

My duty here today is to find some financial papers and bonds that lay somewhere in a pile of boxes in the bedroom closet where they haven't been opened since my parents relocated from New York, but I am hoping to discover some other things—a cartoon of a chubby-faced navigator free-falling through the sky, a Silver Star.

What I'm getting is blue-flower patterned dishes and 3-D pop-up books, tablecloths and gravy boats.

This whole week has been about boxes for me. When I returned to work on Monday I was given an assignment to write about an eccentric artist, or actually this retired businessman named Earl, who is creating art without actually being recognized for it. Museums keep rejecting his work because it is too direct, too forthright. "People understand it," he says. "And that's no good."

He started creating his work in a small storage facility and then just kept renting more and more bays until he had filled over 7,000 square feet. It is all multimedia stuff, some pieces taking up an entire room.

Built like a maze, there was so much to explore, but I couldn't get past a large exhibit near the doorway, where an entire wall was covered with boxes stacked atop one another until they touched the ceiling. The fronts had been cut out of each so you could see the contents inside and each box represented a different period in his life. There was a vintage Pepsi-Cola bottle from the first time he played spin the bottle at age eleven, there was the jarred cancerous prostate gland from when he was seventy-two, there was a scrap of paper summing up his own battle with his mother's deteriorating memory: "The saddest words my mother ever spoke to me were, 'Who are you?' "

A few of the boxes were closed. "Those are for my secrets," he said.

I wondered what Will's and Dad's boxes would look like. I'm not talking about the junk you accumulate over the years but the items and moments that define your lifetime. I am not foolish enough to think I could conjure up what would be in those boxes. I think each of them would have to do it personally, the way this honest and sincere man has done alone here in his warehouse. How many rainy afternoons he contemplated what parts of his existence belonged in the open-faced boxes is not even for me to ask. I have never seen anything so personal.

"You can ask me about myself, but it's all there," Earl said, turning away.

The closest I come to experiencing that side of my father is when I open up a little blue suitcase at the back of the closet and am charmed by its contents. It reminds me of when a child keeps a stash of his favorite stuff in a big shoe box under his bed. There are the plans for his first home, an antique blood pressure instrument, a silver dollar that opens up like a Swiss army knife, his wedding picture, an ancient time card from one of his first jobs, a ripped square from a parachute, the Purple Heart.

After that find I start ripping through the boxes like a madman lusting after significance. There have got to be more boxes teeming with personality and secrets from the past but as I pull the newspaper stuffing out of box after box and toss aside Crock-Pots, napkin holders, and sets of gas-station glasses, I realize I am being silly. None of us could fill so many boxes with sentimental and significant offerings; for any of us, one little blue suitcase is plenty.

What remains is so heavy it must be books, I say to myself as I start stacking some of the larger boxes against a wall without even opening them. As I pull one of the last ones up, it gets away from me and I try to catch the bottom flaps before they let loose but it is too late and I am falling to the ground, tumbling over a pile of elephants.

For a few minutes I sit on the floor among them, running my fingers around the intricate cuts in the hard wood where their sturdy legs bend at the knee. Some are missing their tusks.

I gather up as many as I can and drag them out of my parents' bedroom. When I reach the living room I get a flash of another kind of energy in this place. I see Peter skittering across the hallway in a towel after having taken a vigorous shower in that bathroom like it was some kind of death-affirming baptism, I see Whopper wrappers being discarded, and four Busch beers still on hold. For an instant, I see the living, but even they seem like ghosts.

I hear the words to a song I have never sung. "Oh where do we go now, but nowhere." I check behind me to be sure the double doors are still open. "Do not lock me in here," I say aloud. I have to stick around a few more minutes to wait for a phone call but our family's present situation is palpable, there's no escape.

Peter also went back to work this week and he told me that someone he hadn't seen in a while asked him how his new job is going. "And I went to say, 'Great,' " he said. "But I had to stop myself."

He said he realized that nothing can be "great" anymore because whether it's a job promotion or falling in love or whatever, he can't call his father to say, "Hey, guess what?" He can no longer share things with his father and brother, therefore everything is diminished. "The best anything can ever be now—is good," he said.

My past pillaged, my future robbed. I can't get it out of my head.

I'm perspiring from the pacing so I go to the kitchen to get a glass of tap water. It tastes disgustingly warm and it splashes up onto my shirt as I return to the living room, slam my back against the wall, and slide down to the floor where I am caught in the breeze between the front doors and the patio. Scattered across the worn carpet are the elephants. They are just sitting there, basking in the sun.

Waiting to Be Upgraded

Time, they say.

Time seems to make it worse.

I must go back to those words of faith someone pushed on me in another lifetime. "One day there will be a sign, there will be no denying it and your doubts will be erased forever. You will never be the same."

1. Give me a sign.
2. Erase my doubt.
3. Ensure my unconditional belief.
4. Never be the same.

No, it doesn't quite stack up that way. Only the latter seems to ring true—I will never be the same. Death will do that to you. And I know that I sound like a fool to those who know all too well what death does to you and how you have to persevere.

Someone who became tired of my dwelling on this pulled me aside recently and said, "Hey, you act as if it's the first time anyone ever died."

"It is," I said.

I know very well that just as every birth cannot be a miracle, every death cannot be a tragedy, but I also naively realize that no matter how many people die every day, it is always new to someone. Somebody's always getting a first taste.

And I'm spitting it out.

In the beginning, I appeased myself with thoughts of a kingdom in the clouds. I tried to visualize the pearly gates and beyond, even zoomed in on a mailbox that said WILL on it. But in this case time did work its magic, eventually shoving me back to the reality I guess I chose for myself a long time ago. I don't want nothin' to do with promises of heavens or hells, splashes of holy water, or earthly saints who seem too sure about their God's intentions. I want my brother back.

I want him to at least have the chance to build his own legacy, to at least have the opportunity to become a prince instead of "just a pissa" to those few who knew and loved him.

Because maybe I'm not so sure that there is anything

beyond our little stretch of existence. Maybe I'm not so sure it isn't over the second we slip and crack our heads open. Maybe because it is not out of my realm of possibility to think that his death has absolutely no meaning at all. I guess what I'm saying is, for now, I'm bypassing God.

Not that I don't think it is sad to go through this world only believing in happenstance, circumstance, coincidence, and shit happens. It is sad, it truly is.

But sadness is a place we can sometimes settle into. I understand it and I will not fight it.

It has put a gentle aura around my days of late and it doesn't stop the laughter or cap the energy I need to get through the hours. It has not prevented me from going through the motions. And I know neither hope nor wishful thinking should ever be considered selfish. I needed to be told that just as I need to be continually prodded into making a leap of faith. I sincerely hope it will come some day. I am extremely envious of the true believer.

Sometimes I think maybe it's not that I do not believe in heaven but I am more drawn to—more fascinated and pre-occupied by—the stupid questions we ask, the songs we sing badly, the shelter we take in the sun, the pastry we carefully pick out of a vending machine to ease the pain. I don't need that other world to justify this one.

But it would be nice, wouldn't it?

In the meantime, I have reiterated to my mom that there are still things in life to live for: her surviving children, her grandchildren, *Ally McBeal*.

And I certainly have my own. As do my brothers. There will be no great but we are holding out for good.

"Don't tell anybody but I think I might go see a psychic," Peter said the other day. Looking for answers is still keeping him busy.

I can easily ramble on about things that have been happening lately. For one, I forgot my PIN yesterday.

Also, we've been taking turns driving the Cutlass Supreme that my dad and Will toodled around in during their final days. "Can you drive a dead man's car?" Danny asked. "Is it legal? Is the insurance still good?"

I don't think so, Danny, but who cares?

And speaking of legalities. Will, who was a man of letters, just sent a neatly typed one to the police department last week.

Dear Sirs:

This is not a complaint against the North Palm Beach Police. I just think there was a misunderstanding. I think the North Palm Beach Police are the finest there is and I have a lot of respect for what the officer and the department do in the community. Because of illness in my family (my father is in hospice and my mother is unable to care for herself), I do not want to take time away from my parents and go to court at a time when they need me so much.

So I am going to pay the fine and get the points against my driver's license. But I wanted you to know

I am very disappointed about losing my Safe Driver's License.

> Sincerely,
> William J. Shine

We are very disappointed, too, Will, more than you can ever imagine. And the license I hold in my hand will always say Safe Driver on it.

Will would be pleased to know that Christine has been making replacement tusks out of toothpicks and I am finding homes for most of the elephants. I also find myself staring at the young people in our immediate world: Nicole, Brynn, Dante, and little Daniel. Mesmerized, I can't take my eyes off them and it's not because I am worried that some harm will befall them. Actually, I think it's quite the opposite. I am marveling at the fact that, in my eyes, they will surely live forever.

Death truly does have its own afterlife. I've semi-retired my beeper but calls keep coming in to remind us we're all still entrenched in it. I got a call that the death certificates are in, which we were waiting for to settle some financial matters, and I was like, "Oh, fantastic!" as if it were the photo lab calling to tell me my pictures of the Grand Canyon had just come back.

I am sure there will be plenty of incidents like that to come.

Peter and I had discussed how we were going to become better people from this. How, after we received such compassion from our fellow man during this ordeal we had to return it somehow. "We've been touched," we said. We will become gentle human beings who never have a harsh word for anyone and have such patience that people will be astonished by our saintliness or, at the very least, our civility.

Well, that lasted until about the time we got to the airport on the way back from Arlington and I took a fit that the snack-bar lady only gave me enough cream cheese for half a bagel and wanted to charge me for more.

"Stop, it's just cream cheese," Peter said, delicately shouldering me.

"So, what's your point?" I said.

No, this will not change any of us for the better.

And Peter faltered shortly after when we were at TGIFriday's and the waitress kept bringing him sliced limes that wouldn't fit in the neck of his Corona. "I'm sorry, sir. We have a machine that slices them up and that's how they come out," the waitress said.

"Well, couldn't someone take a knife and slice the lime by hand so it would fit?" he said. "Is that too much to ask?"

That type of incident might sum up everything that is wrong about the service industry in America today but "It's just limes," I said to him.

As I tried to say before: As a whole, the good in family overshadows the bad in each of us.

About a week ago I received a letter from a guy named Mike Redmond whom I went to high school with and roomed with when I first made the move to Florida. We, too, had let time equal distance and hadn't seen each other in ages. He had heard about what happened and was disturbed that I hadn't called him. It had entered my mind. He's a big guy and would have made a great pallbearer but it seemed awkward to start ringing people up and burdening them with such news.

"But how many people really knew Will?" he wrote. "I should have been there."

He is right. One more voice would have been a big addition. He signed his letter "An old friend" and it made me cry a little. For myself, I think.

Anyway, for the record, I have one friend now.

After Arlington, Peter had a few days before he had to be back in New York and he kept pestering me to take him to see the hospice room that my father had spent his final days in. We swept through the atrium to the soft yellow room where someone had taken his place and was sitting up in the bed as still as the small love seat and recliner that adorned the room. "Nice furniture," Peter said.

Before we left they gave us a small bag of his belongings that had been left behind. I reached in and fumbled around like it was a trick-or-treat bag and pulled up Danny's Chieftains CD.

Yesterday, I received a card in the mail from *Reader's Digest*. It said: A ONE-YEAR SUBSCRIPTION IS PRESENTED TO YOU WITH BEST WISHES FROM: DANIEL L. SHINE.

I remember when Dante had a magazine drive to raise money at his school he had sent a catalog to Grandpa a month or two before he became ill to see if he wanted any and I guess he decided that every man needs a subscription to *Reader's Digest,* even if it's only to flap-dry his deodorant. They also include a card you can drop in the mail to show your appreciation. It says: TO: MR. DANIEL L. SHINE. THANK YOU SO MUCH FOR YOUR KINDNESS AND FOR YOUR GIFT.

I will certainly drop it in the mail.

I do less running and more walking these days and the pace seems to make me more aware of my surroundings. At the end of my block the other morning I saw a boy of seven or eight walking a toddler, a younger sibling, by the hand. And though I have no clear memory, it must have been Will who took me by the hand as a child, who got stuck with tugging me across the street. Who looked down on me while I looked up at him.

Thank you, too, Will.

The guys. "Those two guys," is how Danny refers to them now.

You know, there are so many things I don't know. I don't know what it is to toss off an M-16 and watch my true love disappear into the jungles of a foreign land. I don't know what it is to drop a gunner out the trapdoor of a B-17 and then free fall to the earth in a shower of shrapnel.

But I do know what it is to lose "two guys" I truly loved within twenty-four hours.

Today, I take the Cutlass for that ten-minute oil change that had become such a target of concern. And while I wait (for thirty-four minutes) I think about how those days I spent holed up in hospital rooms with Will were like when we were jammed into a small bedroom as kids. I find some solace that we were so close in the beginning and so close in the end, like so many fractured relationships, maybe those are the only times that really matter.

Maybe.

But my heart truly tells me that it is in the middle that we need one another the most. That is the only thing I have learned from this ordeal. It is my regret.

Watching the attendant pour the cool blue windshield washer fluid into the car I think of my father's ocean swims in the turquoise sea, how he would go out 200 yards and do laps like the great Atlantic was a backyard pool.

Hey, I am the fool who's got no closure—I'm living in an open-ended world—and I want to keep fooling myself. So, my father could be out there just beyond the breakers as we speak, and Will, Will could beep me any second . . . from anywhere.

As I pull out, I hit the windshield washers and let the icy blue liquid wash over me; let it keep me from seeing clearly, let it distract me from a simple fact that I will be forever running from.

Life ends.

About the Author

T. M. Shine works for the news and entertainment weekly *City Link* as a feature writer and humor columnist. He lives in Lantana, Florida.

	DATE DUE	

JAMES PRENDERGAST
LIBRARY ASSOCIATION

JAMESTOWN, NEW YORK

Member Of

Chautauqua-Cattaraugus Library System